DEREK LEININGER, PH.D.
WITH COACH CLYDE HART

BREAKING DOWN THE WALL

TRAINING THE HIGH SCHOOL
400 METER RUNNER

Cover design and interior graphics by Jenifer Potter

400Wall.com

Derek Leininger

Breaking Down the Wall: Training the High School 400 Meter Runner

ISBN-10: 8399379739

ISBN-13: 979-8399379739

First published in the United States of America
FIRST EDITION

Acknowledgments

I want to thank Coach Clyde Hart for his contributions to this project. Coach Hart is the best 400 meter coach the world has ever seen. It was an honor and privilege to spend a week with him in Texas in June 2022 and to continue collaborating with him via telephone and email in the months that followed. Every time I talk to him about 400 meter training, I learn something new. He is the best of all time.

I want to thank my wife, Gwen. She has been an amazing thought partner and editor throughout this project. Every important piece of writing I have done in the past 14 years has been improved by her thoughtful advice and editing skills.

I want to thank my older daughter, Georgia, for her persistent excitement throughout this project.

I want to acknowledge my younger daughter, Jane, who was born in the middle of this project.

I want to thank my friend, Brad Peterson, one of the best coaches I know. Brad introduced me to Coach Hart's 400 training 20 years ago when we were coaching together. Brad continues to coach championship runners at every distance, including the 400.

I want to thank my friend, Jenifer Potter, who shared her artistic talents for the cover art and diagrams included in this book.

I want to thank my friend, Tyler Sellhorn, for his sage advice and his encouragement during this project.

I want to thank my friend, Sean Miller, for teaching me about mountain climbing.

Table of Contents

About the Authors

Author: Derek Leininger, Ph.D.
Derek is a former high school track and field and cross country coach. In the early 2000s he found information online about Coach Clyde Hart and how he trained 400 meter runners at Baylor University. Leininger studied Coach Hart's system and modified it for high school athletes. In 2009 Leininger coached the Indiana state runners-up in the boys 4x400 meter relay, and in 2010 he coached the Indiana state champions in the 4x400 meter relay using the balanced approach to training that we present in this book.

Leininger left coaching in 2015 when he became a school administrator, but he continues to stay connected to high school track and field and cross country through his work at IndianaRunner.com and as a meet director, broadcast commentator, and track and field official. Leininger earned his Ph.D. in Educational Administration from Indiana State University in 2019. Leininger is currently a school principal and an adjunct professor in Fort Wayne, Indiana, where he lives with his wife and two daughters.

Collaborator: Coach Clyde Hart
Coach Hart is a retired track and field coach and widely considered the best 400 meter coach in world history. Hart began his coaching career for 6 years at Little Rock Central High School in Little Rock, Arkansas. Hart coached 5 team state champions during his 6-year tenure at Little Rock Central, and his athletes broke every state record, except for one event.

Hart returned to Baylor University, his alma mater, in 1963, where he coached track and field for 56 years, retiring in 2019. During the final phase of his coaching career he also coached professional 400 meter athletes in Waco, Texas.

During his career, Coach Hart had unprecedented success in coaching 400 meter athletes. Hart coached 3 athletes to 4 Olympic gold medals in the 400 meter dash (Michael Johnson in 1996 and 2000, Jeremy Wariner in 2004, and Sanya Richards-Ross in 2012). Hart coached 9 different Olympians and his athletes earned a combined 15 Olympic medals (including 11 gold). He coached athletes to the gold medal in either the 400 meter dash or 4x400 meter relay in six straight Olympics (1992–2012). Hart coached more male athletes to sub-45 second performances and sub-44 second performances than any other coach in history.

Hart coached 20 NCAA championship 4x400 meter relay teams and 6 NCAA champions in the 400 meter dash. Coach Hart's last protégé was Wil London, whom he coached through the 2021 Olympic Trials. Coach Hart lives in Woodway, Texas, with his wife, Maxine.

Coach Clyde Hart's Olympic Medal Winners

1992 Barcelona	Michael Johnson	4x400	Gold
1996 Atlanta	Michael Johnson	200	Gold
1996 Atlanta	Michael Johnson	400	Gold
2000 Sydney	Michael Johnson	400	Gold
2000 Sydney	Greg Haughton	400	Bronze
2000 Sydney	Greg Haughton	4x400	Silver
2004 Athens	Jeremy Wariner	400	Gold
2004 Athens	Jeremy Wariner	4x400	Gold
2004 Athens	Darold Williamson	4x400	Gold
2008 Beijing	Jeremy Wariner	400	Silver
2008 Beijing	Jeremy Wariner	4x400	Gold
2008 Beijing	Sanya Richards	400	Bronze
2008 Beijing	Sanya Richards	4x400	Gold
2012 London	Sanya Richards-Ross	400	Gold
2012 London	Sanya Richards-Ross	4x400	Gold

Purpose

It is a Monday morning in June and I am standing outside the entrance of my hotel in Woodway, Texas. It is only 9 o'clock and the heat is already stifling, something I expected to endure during my summer visit to central Texas. Later in the day, the 101 degree high temperature will fall one degree shy of setting an all-time record. I dress light, wearing sandals, khaki shorts, a dry-fit t-shirt, and a baseball cap as I wait for a red SUV to pick me up. The vehicle approaches and stops. I hop in the passenger seat and I shake hands and introduce myself to Clyde Hart, a man with whom I have been emailing back and forth for months ahead of our scheduled in-person meeting.

Coach Hart pulls away from the hotel and merges on to Highway 84 as we head east toward nearby Baylor University. During the 15 minute car ride to campus Coach remarks about the temperature, saying this is even hotter than normal. He would know. The man has lived in this community for more than 60 years. We arrive at the Baylor University track stadium, situated on the north shore of the Brazos River. Coach is retired but he still has his own parking space, designated by a sign that reads: Reserved for Clyde Hart.

We walk toward a beautiful, state-of-the art, multi-million dollar athletic facility that bears his name, the Clyde Hart Track and Field Stadium. As we walk the halls of the facility, Coach shows me pictures on the wall of the dozens of athletes he coached to NCAA championships and Olympic medals. The walls are lined with picture after picture of athletes and relay teams highlighting the excellence that stretched the span of the past six decades. Coach is humble enough to not point out the bust statue of himself honoring his lifelong commitment to the university and the sport of track and field. The whole thing is surreal. After touring the facility, we make our way to an empty conference room to discuss the topic that we have been emailing back and forth about all spring. In this beautiful, modern track and field stadium we are here to discuss an ancient race. A race that Coach Hart has spent a lifetime studying and perfecting: the 400 meter dash.

The 400 meter dash is iconic, with origins in the Ancient Greek Olympic Games. The Diaulos Race was introduced to the Games in 724 BC. Up to that point, the only foot race was approximately 200 meters, one time around the stadium track. The Diaulos race introduced a two-lap race and the origins of the modern 400 meter dash were born. The event immediately hooked athlete and spectator alike, as the distance required a brutal combination of sprinting ability and endurance to hold near-top speed for the full distance. The event has been included in every Olympic Games ever since, both in the ancient era and in the modern Olympic Games reintroduced in 1896.

Our purpose in writing this book is simple: The 400 meter race has been around for nearly 3,000 years, yet many training plans still fail to include the proper balance of speed and endurance required to truly excel in this event. We see evidence of this at all levels, but particularly in high school where this balanced approach to training is so vital to the long-term development of a young 400 meter athlete. As a former high school 400 meter coach, I found Coach Hart's training materials online and I modified them to fit high school athletes. The results were amazing, culminating in a state runner-up and a state championship in the 4x400 meter relay and two state runner-up finishes in the 4x800 meter relay in my home state of Indiana.

Coach Hart and I have both observed a decline in 400 meter dash performances due to insufficient training. Numerous advances in exercise science research over the past 30 years are still not reflected in many high school 400 meter training programs. I reached out to Coach Hart and he agreed to collaborate on this book project to present training concepts that are research-based and have proven to be successful over many years with numerous athletes. The concepts in this book have resulted in achievements at the highest level, including world records and Olympic gold medals.

There are no secrets. Unlike other sports, track and field coaches, generally speaking, have always been willing to share their ideas with each other. We are hoping to contribute to that greater library of knowledge, specifically for 400 meter training. Coaches today are fortunate to possess an abundance of information. As Coach Hart puts it, "You have more information and tools for coaching on your phones today than I had in my first 30 years of coaching." We write this book as a collection of training ideas that we wish we would have possessed early in our coaching careers.

Training theory for the 400 meter dash has improved dramatically over the past 30 years. We have more knowledge and scientific research to show us how we ought to train athletes. We observe that many coaches do not understand this shift and, thus, are still training 400 meter athletes the same way that we did half a century ago. These philosophies for training 400 meter runners are neither scientifically sound nor are they producing consistent results. Some coaches today are doubling down on low-volume, high-intensity training methods. This methodology is simply outdated, modern research does not support it. In alignment with modern research, we advocate for a balanced approach to training 400 meter runners that incorporates both aerobic and anaerobic development.

In a way, coaches are like chefs. A novice can follow a recipe and replicate something that looks and tastes very similar to the original menu item. A master chef will learn, over time, how and why to adjust the recipe; they will customize and improve it to become something even better. Our goal is to provide enough information in this book to give you, the coach, some guidelines (a recipe, if you will), and then you will be able to customize it to fit your needs and become that master chef.

Voice of the Book

The goal for this book is to make the "voice" feel like a coach-to-coach conversation. Coach Hart and I spent a week together in Waco, Texas, in June 2022 having these conversations—in the Baylor University track and field offices, on the patio in his backyard, and sitting together at his dining room table. My goal was to write this book in a way that allows the reader to *listen in* on those conversations.

The presentation of the material is sometimes complicated because I combine the voice of the author (Derek Leininger) and collaborator (Coach Clyde Hart). Many of the ideas originate from Coach Hart and his decades of experience coaching track and field, but the voice is often first person plural ("we") because these are concepts that we both fully believe. At times when I describe a specific story that Coach Hart shared, I change the voice to third person pronouns to make it clear that this particular idea comes from Coach. At times when I describe an experience unique to me I use first person pronouns.

Very few ideas in coaching are truly unique. We all borrow and steal ideas from others, we follow the current research, and we observe what works and does not work within our own coaching style and with our athletes. Some of the ideas in this book are ideas that originated from others, and we try to give proper credit to those individuals. This book is a collection of ideas that are *keepers*, concepts and workouts that stood the test of time and produced excellent results year after year.

I try to explain the science in clear terms. In the science and physiology section, I get admittedly nerdy with the scientific terminology, but I want to demonstrate to the reader that this program is based on sound scientific principles. We use the same scientific terminology that exercise scientists use to show that this balanced program is rooted in research. Everywhere else in the book I maintain that coach-to-coach voice.

Old School is New School

Some critics of a balanced training program for 400 meter runners suggest that this is an "old school" way of training. The implication is that newer training programs focus primarily on speed development and provide newer, better ways to train 400 meter athletes. Truth be told, we are actually "new school" in that our training program is consistent with all the scientific research over the past 30 years regarding aerobic versus anaerobic percentages and contributions to the 400 meter dash. Fifty years ago coaches focused primarily on speed development because exercise scientists at that time suggested that the 400 meter dash was 90% anaerobic and only 10% aerobic. We now know that these percentages are actually 60% anaerobic and 40% aerobic. The balanced training approach that we recommend is consistent with modern research. To focus solely on speed development with very little endurance emphasis is an outdated model; those who coach this way are reverting back to the training models of 50+ years ago, which have been proven to be ineffective.

A key attribute of any coach and any training program is continual self-evaluation to find areas for improvement. We should always strive to get better. Get 1% better, get 5% better, just keep making improvements year after year. Coaches who never change their training program are the ones with the old school mindset. They are stuck in their ways without results to back them up. Coaches should be like teachers or medical professionals; these are jobs that require staying current with modern research and the best practices within their field.

The training system that we present in this book is tried and true and it is the result of decades of self-evaluation and improvement. It has worked in the past and it continues to work today. In the mens 400 meter dash in world history, there have been 90 performances by 22 athletes in which the athlete ran faster than 44 seconds. The most common name on this list is Michael Johnson, who broke 44 seconds on 22 different occasions! The second most common name on this list is Jeremy Wariner, who broke 44 seconds on 9 different occasions; Wariner is tied with another athlete for #2 (WorldAthletics.org). Johnson and Wariner were both exclusively coached by Clyde Hart during their collegiate and professional running careers.

We understand why critics would try to negatively classify our training approach as old school and outdated. Indeed, you will hear us promote the classic advice that there is no substitute for hard work and not everyone is willing to accept the reality of what it takes to be an elite 400 meter coach or athlete. But hard work is not outdated. The evidence is clear: this balanced training program is consistent with current exercise science research and it has produced success at the absolute highest level.

Do Not be a River Person

Over the years Coach Hart has observed that many people are like a river. Just like the flow of a river, they take the path of least resistance. The training program that we outline in this book is challenging, both as a coach and athlete. We are not sadistic, we are not offering a harder program just for the sake of it being harder. We offer you a program that works.

Winning requires a willingness to work harder and smarter than your opponents. Champions understand this, and they accept this reality long before becoming champions; that is why they finish atop the podium. Michael Johnson accepted this in the early 1990s, and by the end of the decade he had earned 16 gold medals (4 in the Olympics, 8 in World Championships, and 4 in the Goodwill Games).

Baylor athletes Jeremy Wariner and Darold Williamson understood this. They watched the hard work and the results of Johnson and Coach Hart over the previous decade and they decided it was their turn for Olympic glory when they earned gold medals in 2004 in the 400 meter dash (Wariner) and 4x400 meter relay. Sanya Richards-Ross understood this after watching Wariner and Williamson dominate the 2004 Olympics. In the years that followed, Richards-Ross decided to train with Coach Hart and in 2012 she had her own Olympic gold medal moment in the 400.

Some coaches preach a false gospel of easy training. They pretend that athletes can run short, fast workouts all the time and magically achieve great 400 meter performances. That is simply not true. It is not aligned with the exercise science and it certainly is not producing consistent success in 400 meter athletes.

Your athletes are capable of working harder, but it will take a shift in mindset by the coach and athlete. Do not put limitations on your athletes just because somebody tries to convince you that quality aerobic workouts are too hard or unnecessary for your athletes. A balanced training program is the only way to consistently produce championship 400 meter runners.

As a coach, do the harder and better training. Convince your athletes to do harder and better training. This is the only path to ultimate success. A river looks for shortcuts, but as the next section shows, there are none.

Evaluating Training Advice

Plenty of training programs will offer you advice on how to prepare athletes for the 400 meter dash. Conduct a quick online search and you will find articles and videos of various 400 meter training programs. Some will have similarities to what you read in this book, other programs will be very different. When you evaluate the merits of a 400 meter training program, you should seek to answer two primary questions.

Question 1: Does this training program align with current research? The 400 meter dash is an endurance sprint event that is approximately 60% anaerobic and 40% aerobic. When you evaluate the entirety of a 400 meter training program, you should consider whether the program is adequately addressing both the aerobic and anaerobic components of the event. If you see a training program that is composed entirely of distance running (aerobic), you can quickly rule that out as a viable 400 meter training program. Conversely, if you see a training program that is composed almost entirely of short sprinting, you can also rule that out as a viable 400 meter training program. You should be looking for a balanced approach that addresses high quality training for both energy systems.

Question 2: Does this training program produce results? There is an old saying: the proof is in the pudding. At the risk of sounding too obvious, you can determine the quality and consistency of results that are being produced by coaches and athletes using a particular training program. Replication is key. If a coach inherits a supremely talented athlete at the high school level, almost anything they do in training will result in the athlete winning many races. However, a coach that is implementing a balanced 400 meter training program will be able to replicate success year after year in both the 400 meter dash and 4x400 meter relay.

It is a red flag if a coach tells you they have the recipe for success but they have only coached one elite athlete. Relay success is a better indicator than individual success because 4x400 success requires the coach to produce success with a larger sample size. A training program worth implementing should already have a proven track record of success over multiple years with multiple athletes and relays. The coach presenting the training program should have already proven that they can replicate success within their own team if you have any hopes of replicating success with your athletes.

Some training programs are selling you a shortcut that will never work. Some coaches will try to tell you that your athletes can be successful in the 400 meter dash without creating an aerobic (endurance) base. It sounds enticing, but it is fool's gold. The best coaches and athletes will accept this difficult truth and they will put in the work required to be champions. Others will look for shortcuts that, unfortunately for them, will always lead to dead ends.

FOUR KEY PRINCIPLES OF TRAINING

"As to methods, there may be a million and then some, but principles are few. The man who grasps principles can successfully select his own methods. The man who tries methods, ignoring principles, is sure to have trouble."

This quote comes from Harrington Emerson, a business theorist and efficiency engineer in the United States in the late 1800s and early 1900s. Emerson spent much of his professional career studying how to help employers and employees perform better and more efficiently in their work.

Emerson's words highlight a concept that is foundational to how we approach training 400 meter athletes. Later in the book we provide you with numerous and very specific examples of methods. We provide you with the exact training plan and workouts that have produced numerous NCAA, American, and Olympic champions in the 400 meter event. The training program outlined in this book is, quite simply, the most successful and proven 400 meter training program in the history of the world. Coach Clyde Hart's coaching résumé for 400 meter athletes is unrivaled. As the kids say, he is the GOAT: Greatest of All Time.

Having said that, there are four key principles to discuss before we get into specific workout details. These principles are the foundation that these workouts are built upon. If you skip over these principles and rush straight to the methods, you will lack the base knowledge to understand *why* the methods work so well. You will also lack the understanding needed to properly adjust the methods when needed. To quote Emerson again, you will be "sure to have trouble."

Training is not merely implementing a prescribed set of workouts. It is about why you are doing something, how you do it, and understanding when to adjust it. You can take specific workout ideas from this book and accept them or reject them. We are fine either way. But make sure you understand the supporting principles for your training program. You should be able to explain to your athletes exactly why each workout is going to help them improve as a 400 meter runner.

Principle #1: The 40 Second Wall

Click your stopwatch and wait for it. The most dramatic moment in a 400 meter dash happens at 40 seconds. This is the dreaded wall. For collegiate and professional male athletes, they will reach 40 seconds somewhere around 350 meters. Many high school runners will reach 40 seconds somewhere between 275–325 meters. Close, competitive 400 meter races are always won (and lost) after 40 seconds.

Consider this: You watch a high school 400 meter race and an athlete in an outside lane gets out aggressively through the first 200 meters. Nobody has made up the stagger on them yet, so they continue to drive hard through the curve, but by the time they near the homestretch you can see that something is wrong. Their stride length decreases and their smooth rhythm turns choppy and tight. Their arms appear to have doubled in weight as the athlete struggles to pump them to support their failing leg muscles. You watch painfully as one, two, three athletes and then eventually most of the field passes them on the homestretch. You just watched the runner hit the 40 second wall. I have watched this exact scenario play out hundreds of times during my time as an athlete, coach, and commentator. It is always painful to watch.

So, what just happened? It is actually very scientific and predictable, and it demonstrates how the different energy systems work together to support your maximal effort for one lap around the track. We will cover these scientific components in more detail in the next section of the book. To put it simply: Your body is not designed to sprint all out for 400 meters because nobody can run 400 meters under 40 seconds. After 40 seconds the athlete has depleted their body of the anaerobic energy needed to run at this near-maximal pace. Without the proper balance of aerobic and anaerobic training, it becomes impossible for the athlete to maintain a fast pace beyond 40 seconds.

While the 40 second wall applies to everyone, it is even more consequential for high school athletes than it is for collegiate athletes, simply because it takes high school athletes longer to run 400 meters. An elite collegiate male athlete who runs 45 seconds will only have to run 5 seconds beyond 40. A high school athlete running 60 seconds will have 20 seconds to contend with beyond 40. A balanced training approach is even more important for high school athletes because they have to deal with a longer period of racing beyond 40 seconds. The better aerobic shape you are in, the better your body will be at handling lactate buildup late in the race as your anaerobic system taps out and your aerobic system takes over. In a close race, that will make all the difference.

When you run nearly all out in the 400 meter dash, your body adapts by using glucose in the body to produce anaerobic energy, but that fuel burns very quickly. It is like throwing kindling into a campfire. It will burn and quickly produce fire, but once it burns out it is gone. To sustain a fire, you need bigger logs with more substance.

Take heart, there is good news. When coaches understand the science behind this 40 second wall, they can train their athletes to be prepared for the reality they will face in the homestretch. After all, not every athlete rigs up and fades at the end of the race. Some athletes train and race properly, and they are the athletes passing everyone else on the homestretch.

NASCAR Gas Tanks
In NASCAR, each competing vehicle uses 104-Octane fuel and each vehicle is limited to a 22-gallon gas tank. When cars refill, the fuel comes from a central tank that all competitors use to prevent teams from adding anything to the fuel. The fuel itself and the gas tanks are designed to make sure that each vehicle can only go the same distance down the track before they run out of gas. Imagine, for a moment, if a car was allowed to have a 30-gallon gas tank. What an advantage that would be to get further along in the race before having to refuel. That is the advantage that athletes have when they use a balanced training approach for 400 meters.

Principle #2: The 60/40 Ratio

60/40 is the New 90/10
The 400 meter dash is what most people call an endurance sprint event. Just like the oxymoron that describes it, the 400 is a complex event. However, the complex energy demands of the event have not changed in thousands of years. An athlete lining up in Olympia, Greece in 724 BC faced the same grueling task that an athlete lining up in Paris, France in the 2024 Olympics will face. The biggest difference is that we have finally developed high-quality, reliable research methods that allow us to better understand this event.

Research over the past 30 years has proven that the 400 meter dash relies approximately 60% on the runner's anaerobic system and 40% on the aerobic system. Fifty years ago most people believed these ratios for the 400 were 90% anaerobic and only 10% aerobic. Coaches trained their athletes during that era reflecting this 90/10 belief. They prescribed a lot of short speed training with very little emphasis on developing aerobic strength or endurance.

We will explain aerobic and anaerobic energy systems in more detail later, but here is an overly simplistic explanation: Aerobic is the endurance energy needed to hold a steady pace. Anaerobic is the speed energy that is needed when an athlete runs really fast.

This is actually great news for many athletes. This is not like the 100 meter dash, where the athlete with the better natural speed almost always wins the race. In the 400 meter dash there is a much larger aerobic component to the event, which means there is more room for improvement for coaches and athletes who train with a balanced approach. Late in the race speed is useless and endurance is essential.

Michael Johnson's 1990 Season
Coach Hart began developing this 60/40 approach in the 1980s, and it was confirmed in his mind in 1990 with his star runner Michael Johnson. Johnson suffered a series of injuries that interrupted

multiple seasons while he was a college runner at Baylor University. Coach Hart decided to transition to more aerobic training with Johnson in an effort to keep him healthy. They found that Johnson started running his best results with far less anaerobic training. Coach did not need researchers to tell him that he had hit on something when Johnson was running better than ever after this increase in aerobic training.

Coach Hart and Johnson were planning to go back to more anaerobic training later in the season, but they never got away from this increased aerobic approach once they saw the results. That March, Johnson was running phenomenal times and looked great in training. As Coach Hart explained it, "everything was better." When they looked at Johnson's training percentages, his weekly workout volume was very close to 60% anaerobic and 40% aerobic, which was a much higher aerobic percentage than Johnson had done in prior seasons. After reevaluating, they decided to stay the course.

You can probably guess what happened. Johnson stayed healthy and strong and had his best collegiate season, culminating in NCAA outdoor championships in the 200 meter dash and 4x400 meter relay. He went on to have an amazing summer season after NCAAs, setting a PR of 19.85 in the 200 meter dash and running the world's top six fastest 200 meter performances that season. He also ran three of the world's fastest five performances in the 400 meter dash, setting a new PR of 44.21. Michael emerged as the number one 200 meter runner in the world after running a higher percentage of aerobic work than he had ever done before.

That season was a watershed moment for Coach Hart. After Michael responded so well to this new 60/40 approach, Coach permanently moved his training plan for all of his 400 meter athletes to align closer to 60/40 throughout the competitive season. This plan proved successful with many other athletes and as they say, the rest is history. Baylor would go on to win the outdoor NCAA title in the 4x400 meter relay 9 times between 1990–2008 following this 60/40 approach.

Research Catches Up

During the 1990s researchers began to identify that the aerobic component of almost all track events was higher than previously assumed. This was particularly true in the 400 meter dash. By the end of the decade, Martin and Coe (1997) published ratios of 70% anaerobic and 30% aerobic. Then around the turn of the century, multiple researchers confirmed that the 60/40 percentages that Coach Hart developed a decade prior were exactly right. It turned out that energy contributions to the 400 meter dash were far more aerobic than almost anyone (coaches and exercise scientists alike) previously believed. Spencer and Gastin put it best in their 2001 study: "These results suggest that the relative contribution of the aerobic energy system during track running events is considerable and greater than traditionally thought" (p. 157).

Research Studies in 1990s About Anaerobic & Aerobic Demands in 400 Meter Dash		
Study (Authors, Year)	% Anaerobic	% Aerobic
Lacour et al. (1990)	72%	28%
van Ingen Schenau et al. (1991)	83%	17%
Newsholme et al. (1992)	75%	25%
Martin & Coe (1997)	70%	30%

Table 1: This chart demonstrates the scientific belief in the 1990s that the 400 meter dash was overwhelmingly anaerobic. You can see a gradual shift toward higher aerobic percentages, up to 30% by 1997.

The aerobic percentage is even higher among female athletes (more like 45%) since they spend several seconds longer to complete the 400 meter distance, thus making the aerobic demands slightly higher. This slightly higher aerobic percentage would also apply to high school runners since they are typically running 50-60+ seconds, as compared to the 45-50 second athletes who participated in many of these studies.

Research Studies in Late 1990s and Early 2000s About Anaerobic & Aerobic Demands in the 400 Meter Dash		
Study (Authors, Year)	% Anaerobic	% Aerobic
Hill (1999)	63%	37%
Spencer & Gastin (2001)	57%	43%
Duffield et al. (2005)	59% (men) 55% (women)	41% (men) 45% (women)
van Someren (2006)	62%	38%

Table 2: By the late 1990s and early 2000s exercise scientists learned that the aerobic component was higher than previously though. You can see these numbers represent the 60/40 ratio that we acknowledge today.

Training Should Reflect the 60/40 Principle
The overarching principle here is that your training program should reflect the scientific reality that 40% (or more) of the energy your athlete needs in the 400 meter dash is aerobic. If you are prescribing primarily short, fast sprints and you rarely work on the endurance component, you are not adequately training your athletes for this event.

Principle #3: Quantity to Quality

Jack Patterson was Clyde Hart's college coach at Baylor University in the 1950s. When Coach Hart began his first track and field coaching position at Little Rock High School in Little Rock, Arkansas, in 1957, he called Coach Patterson and asked him to explain his philosophy on coaching. Patterson simply answered, "Quantity to Quality. That is it. If you plan your workouts based on that belief, you will not get into any trouble."

The phrase *quantity to quality* describes the year-long approach to training. In the beginning of the season you have to establish a foundation of aerobic conditioning (quantity) for your athletes before you can introduce faster intervals (quality). In college, this quantity phase begins with the fall training phase in September. In high school, this might more realistically be November or December, once fall sports are finished. In the beginning of the year-long training plan, the majority of your work is going to be aerobic in nature. We suggest beginning these first 2–3 weeks with 90% of your weekly volume of running to be aerobic and then gradually, month by month, move to where you are eventually at 40% aerobic. You are establishing the oxygen delivery system and general conditioning that the athletes need so that their bodies are prepared to 1) handle the length and rigor of the track season and 2) gradually increase in intensity throughout the entire season.

One word of caution: Do not try to move from *quantity to quality* too quickly. The base of the pyramid is the foundation, and it cannot be rushed. Without that proper foundation the athlete is more susceptible to injuries and hitting a plateau in results during the competitive season.

Rest Time between Intervals
One way to make track interval workouts more aerobic is to decrease recovery time. For example, instead of 5 minutes rest, shorten the recovery time to 3 minutes. This will do two key things. First, it will allow the athlete to strike a better balance of anaerobic

to aerobic ratios within that workout, which will align closer with the 60/40 target. Second, it will allow the athlete to run more repetitions. The athletes will not be able to run as fast during this workout, so naturally they will run slightly slower repetitions, but this will allow them to get in more volume.

Point of Clarification

The phrase *quantity to quality* is similar to what some people call a *long to short approach* but we see a subtle difference in the two phrases. Long to short is too simplistic; it would indicate that you do not do anything short and fast early in your training season and, conversely, that you do not do anything long later in the season. That is where we diverge. We recommend doing some short, fast anaerobic work early in the season and we are still doing some aerobic work deep into the competitive season. Long to short is not the worst way to characterize our training program, but *quantity to quality* spells it better.

Weekly Volume Percentages

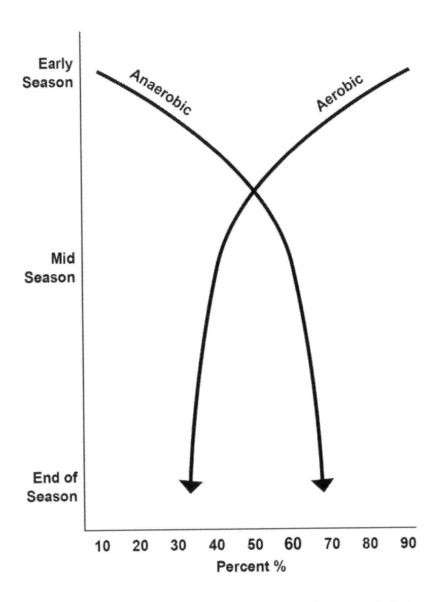

Diagram 1: This diagram shows the *quantity to quality* approach that we recommend. Athletes should begin with 90% aerobic work initially and then gradually increase anaerobic work throughout the season.

Principle #4: Reloading (Peaking is a Myth)

One thing we do not understand is when coaches pick a specific date and say that this date is when their athletes to be in their best shape. That is an admirable goal, but it is nearly impossible in reality. We suggest that peaking is a myth and that your best approach as a coach is to continue to "reload" and help your athletes move to higher levels of fitness and competitive preparedness throughout the season. To prevent plateaus and stagnant results throughout the season you need to schedule specific weeks where you back off the anaerobic work and go back to slightly more aerobic volume. This approach allows you to continue to reach higher levels of both aerobic and anaerobic fitness and, thus, faster 400 meter performances. This is what we mean by reloading.

Imagine you are climbing a mountain and as you get higher in altitude, there is so much cloud cover that you cannot see more than a couple hundred feet up the mountain in front of you. Where is the exact peak of the mountain? You have a general idea of how far you have gone and how much further you have remaining, but you cannot see precisely where the peak of the mountain is. That is the same challenge that we have if we are saying that all of our training is pointing to one specific date or event. It is elusive and it will likely cause you to mis-time your training schedule. You will hold your athletes back at the wrong time and lose opportunities for them to improve their fitness.

An illustration that we believe is accurate and helpful are the ancient Egyptian pyramids. The earliest Egyptian pyramids were built as step pyramids. They were not smooth and they did not go straight up the edge to a clear peak at the top. Rather, these pyramids were built one level at a time and if you were to climb them, you would have to clear one level and then move laterally before climbing the next level. You cannot just race up the side of the pyramid, you have to pause after each level to reset before you attempt the next level.

This is a perfect illustration of how training progressions actually work and what we refer to as reloading.

When we get to the competitive phase of the season athletes are racing consistently and their training volume is more anaerobic than aerobic. In fact, during this part of the season we recommend that many of your weeks will be as high as 70% anaerobic and only 30% aerobic. However, we never want to go more than 3 weeks without scheduling a reloading week. During this reloading week we replace some of the anaerobic work with aerobic work to ensure that the athlete continues to maintain and develop their aerobic energy system. We back off from 70/30 and hit one week at 60/40, then we return to 70/30 for two more weeks. The tendency during the competitive stage is to do all quality and forget about quantity, but that approach is harmful to the athlete because 40% or more of the energy they need for the 400 meter dash is aerobic.

Some coaches have developed an elaborate tapering system where they spend several weeks cutting back and preparing to peak at the right time. During that time, they are holding their athletes back when they do not need to. The athlete's aerobic fitness erodes during that taper and it prevents them from competing their best in the championship races.

Reloading in Action
Athletes who ran under Coach Hart proved time and again that this reloading principle works. In addition to all of the Olympic gold medals (late summer), Coach Hart's athletes also set their best times late in the season. Michael Johnson set the world record in the 200 at the Olympics and the 400 at the World Championships. Sanya Richards-Ross set her American record in the 400 at the World Cup in September. Under Coach Hart, Baylor won the NCAA 4x400 National Championship 20 times. These are all evidence that the reloading principle works. Athletes ran their best times at the very end of the season.

Jeremy Wariner's 2004 season is a perfect example of how the reloading principle works. Wariner won the NCAA Indoor Championship in March and set the world's fastest indoor 400 time that year (45.39 seconds). Wariner continued to improve and won the NCAA Outdoor Championship in June. He then went through the Olympic Trials, a competitive summer schedule, and he was still able to win the Olympic Finals in late August, running his best time of the season. He was able to reload, reload, reload, and he continued to gain fitness all the way to the end of the summer.

Later in the season the athlete will get a lot of their aerobic work through warm ups, cool downs, overdistance intervals, and 200 intervals. The aerobic work looks different in May than it does in the fall, both in percentages and in the type of workouts that you quantify as aerobic.

High School Adjustment
If you have a particularly short season (February–May, for example) then you will end up spending a fair amount of your training season building up the athletes' endurance. In this case, it does not make sense to reload every 3 weeks because you are still building your base. With such a short season, you could adjust and set a mid-season point to reload (or strategically build in two reloading weeks at different points in the season). The reloading concept still applies. You still need to hold your aerobic strength all the way through the season, but since the season is so much shorter you need to prioritize building your base and then determine how many reloading weeks you need to incorporate.

Egyptian Step Pyramids (Reloading)

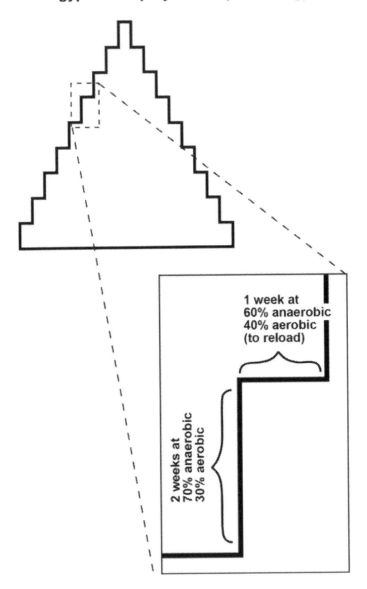

1 week at 60% anaerobic 40% aerobic (to reload)

2 weeks at 70% anaerobic 30% aerobic

Diagram 2: This pyramid shows the reloading principle that we recommend. Athletes do two weeks of 70% anaerobic / 30% aerobic work and then the third week is a reloading week, back to 60% anaerobic / 40% aerobic.

SCIENCE AND PHYSIOLOGY

We briefly outline the science and physiology of the 400 meter dash, but we present the information to you in a practical way. We are not exercise scientists; we are coaches. We want to understand the science and research well enough to confidently build a training program that makes sense. We use the specific scientific terms that exercise scientists use so that we are all using the same terminology.

In this book, I cite 19 different peer-reviewed, published research studies about 400 meter training and racing. The information from these studies completely support our balanced approach to training, but we do not just hand pick sources that happen to agree with us. Truth it, virtually all of the researchers come to the same conclusion. I cannot find any contemporary studies that present significantly different data or findings. Everyone agrees that the 400 meter dash is more aerobic than we ever thought possible prior to the 1990s.

There are Two Labs

When it comes to training athletes, there are two laboratories that a coach should consider. Lab 1 belongs to the exercise scientists. Exercise scientists study human performance in controlled environments using highly scientific tools and procedures. Over time, exercise scientists have become better at measuring and understanding what is happening in the body at various track distances. Coaches today have an abundance of research and scientific data available to them; our collective knowledge and vocabulary is so much greater than it was a few decades ago. If you are a coach, you would be foolish to ignore Lab 1.

There is a second lab that you also need to pay attention to. This lab is the track itself and it belongs to the coaches and the athletes. Lab 1 explains human performance within a vacuum where every variable can be controlled and measured. But that is not the real world in which we live, train, and race. There are certain scientific principles that apply to everyone, but not every athlete is exactly the same. Lab 2 is where coaches study, observe, communicate with, and evaluate *their* athletes continually to tailor their training plan.

Coach Hart has always been intrigued by both labs. Sometimes he would implement an idea that he read from a scientific study, but he abandoned it because it simply did not work. The best ideas must be proven in both labs. There are two labs and great coaches learn how to combine data from both labs to meet the training needs of their athletes. In this section of the book I write a lot about Lab 1.

Interestingly enough, when it comes to breakthroughs in training theory, sometimes Lab 1 leads the way and sometimes Lab 2 is the frontrunner. Often times, Lab 1 is the catalyst. Over time, researchers have improved their methodology and data collection procedures, which has led to better information for coaches to apply to training. Sometimes Lab 2 leads the way, where a coach identifies something well before the researchers. A great example is in *quantity to quality*, one of our four key principles. Coach Jack

Patterson was at Baylor 70 years ago coaching athletes with his *quantity to quality* approach. Recently, Sökmen et al. (2018) conducted research on how to properly train athletes and they identified that endurance training early in the season and then gradual movement toward more speed training later in the season produced optimal results in athlete improvement. Sökmen et al. were not the first or only researchers to recommend this approach, but this is a great example of how a coach *knew* he was right a long time ago and exercise scientists proved him right in the years that followed.

ATP, Aerobic and Anaerobic

ATP

ATP is Adenosine Triphosphate. It is a source of energy at the cellular level. Whenever we run, or engage in physical activity of any kind, we move and contract our muscles. ATP is the sole energy source for this muscle contraction. But humans have a major problem: Our bodies have a very small amount of ATP stored at any given time. Very small. In fact, we only have about 3 grams of ATP immediately available to us, which will only last a matter of seconds when we do any kind of explosive muscle movement, like sprinting.

Physical exercise requires a constant supply of ATP. Our bodies have to constantly generate more ATP to provide energy for our muscles to continue working. This process of generating ATP can be either aerobic or anaerobic. Aerobic is a slower process, but highly efficient. Anaerobic is a much quicker process, but highly inefficient.

Aerobic

By definition, aerobic means *with oxygen*. When we refer to the aerobic energy system, we are referring to our bodies converting glucose into ATP in the presence of an ample supply of oxygen. When we engage in a workout that is highly aerobic, such as walking or slow jogging, our bodies are able to produce ATP at a rate that keeps up with the amount of energy our bodies need. It is like you are using your phone and charging it at the same time, so you never run out of battery. In aerobic creation of ATP, the glucose is broken down fully and the major byproducts are water and carbon dioxide. Water is not harmful and our bodies get rid of the carbon dioxide immediately, through exhaling.

As mentioned above, the body can create ATP aerobically with high efficiency. Obviously, our bodies do get tired, even at low-level activity like walking, but that is rarely because of inadequate amounts of ATP. That typically has more to do with muscular fatigue. If our muscles can handle the effort, our bodies can continue to supply ATP for incredibly long periods of exercise because our bodies have large supplies of glucose that can be converted into ATP. Ultra marathoners are a perfect example of just how long our bodies can produce ATP as a fuel for physical activity.

Anaerobic

By definition, anaerobic means *without oxygen*. When we run very fast, our body demands more energy than we can supply through oxygen alone. When we refer to the anaerobic energy system, we are referring to our bodies converting glucose into ATP using a different process altogether. The faster and shorter we run, the more we rely on our anaerobic system for energy. The major problem is that when our bodies generate ATP anaerobically, the glucose is only partially broken down and because of that we end up with a byproduct at the cellular level called lactate. As this lactate builds up in the cells it limits the muscles' ability to maintain that same high level of effort. Simply put, an increased concentration of blood lactate levels causes the athlete to slow down considerably after about 30–40 seconds of near-maximal speed. That is our 40 second wall, and it is absolutely crucial for 400 meter runners.

Lactate or Lactic Acid?

Many coaches will interchangeably use the terms lactate and lactic acid. An exercise scientist would not appreciate this, but those of us in the real world are talking about the same thing, so to us this is just semantics. Technically, lactic acid is produced by muscle tissue and red blood cells and it is the combination of lactate and hydrogen ions. We will consistently use "lactate" because that is specifically what we are referring to with the 400 meter dash. When you run really hard for 30–120 seconds, your blood lactate concentration increases significantly and will stay elevated for up to 8 minutes after you are done. That higher concentration of blood lactate is what we are interested in, and that is what we refer to throughout this book when we talk about lactate levels.

Aerobic and Anaerobic Combination

Every running event in track requires some combination of aerobic and anaerobic energy systems. The shortest outdoor track event (100 meter dash) requires approximately 80% anaerobic energy, while the longest outdoor track event (10,000 meter run) requires 98% aerobic energy. Training for the short sprints (200 meters and lower) and the distance races (1500 meters and above) are more straightforward. Coaches know that a vast majority of your training should be anaerobic for short sprinters and aerobic for long distance runners.

The two events that are more difficult are the 400 meter and 800 meter events, as the 400 is 60/40 anaerobic and the 800 is 60/40 aerobic. In my opinion, these are the two most complex races for track coaches to navigate because you must constantly evaluate your training program to ensure that you are taking a balanced approach and prescribing the correct ratio of aerobic and anaerobic work for your athletes.

Six Seconds of Free Energy

During the first six seconds of any race the athlete has a brief period of "free" energy at their disposal. During these magical six seconds, the athlete's body uses what is called the ATP–CP system (Adenosine Triphosphate–Creatine Phosphate). This is also sometimes referred to as the Phosphagen System. This system of anaerobic metabolism only lasts about six seconds.

The athlete's body uses Creatine Phosphate to produce ATP, which generates energy immediately but very briefly. During these six seconds the athlete's body is relying 100% on this ATP–CP system for its energy. The athlete's body is not generating any sort of lactate buildup or Hydrogen ions during this time. This is why we refer to it as free energy. No matter how hard the athlete runs in these first six seconds, they are not burning any of the fuel they will need later in the race. Have fun, go out hard, and take advantage of this. Do not try to save anything in these first 6 seconds.

As you may know, lactate buildup is bad news for sprinters. It is like Superman's Kryptonite, causing otherwise strong muscles to feel very weak, very quickly. It leads to a rapid decrease in the athlete's ability to run fast, which is basically the only thing sprinters are interested in doing. If the first two paragraphs are too nerdy for you, that is fine. Just read and understand the final paragraph below.

The implications for sprinters are crystal clear. Whatever sprint race an athlete is competing in, they should always explode out of the blocks and accelerate as fast as they can to top speed over the first six seconds (roughly 50 meters for many athletes). The athlete has six seconds of free energy and they do not want to waste it. The specific implications for the 400 meter runner is that they have free energy for these first six seconds and then they need to "settle in" and find their race pace at that point.

Anaerobic Glycolysis

We already explained about the ATP–CP system. In that system, the athlete uses Creatine Phosphate to generate ATP. This energy is immediately available but only lasts about six seconds. After this ATP–CP system runs out the athlete then relies on the next form of anaerobic energy, the anaerobic glycolytic system.

The anaerobic glycolytic system is when the athlete's body converts glucose in their cells into ATP without enough oxygen to properly sustain that. This happens relatively quickly, but with great complexity, and the body has a very hard time "keeping up" when running very fast and using incredible amounts of energy. Like a high octane race car, the glycolytic system uses fuel that burns very quickly and creates a nasty byproduct.

The first 6 seconds the athlete's body uses the ATP–CP system and then from 6 to 30–40 seconds the athlete relies primarily on this glycolytic system. This is the 40 second wall that we mentioned earlier. After 40 seconds of near-maximal running effort, your glycolytic system can no longer produce energy as fast as you are consuming it. After 30–40 seconds at near-maximal speed, the athlete begins to experience increased lactate levels that force them to slow down immediately. Cicchella (2022) very poignantly refers to this as "lactate intoxication" (p. 7).

Aerobic Contribution

As we have mentioned previously, the energy demands of the 400 meter dash are 60% anaerobic and 40% aerobic. During this stage of anaerobic glycolysis, the athlete is increasingly depending on their aerobic system to provide them with adequate energy. From the 30 second mark to the end of the race, the athlete is depending *primarily* on aerobic energy (Spencer & Gastin, 2001) because at these extreme speeds the anaerobic system taps out by 40 seconds. The longer the athlete takes to run 400 meters, the more aerobic energy they depend on during this final stretch of the race.

Gender Differences

In virtually every research study conducted by exercise scientists, they identified the aerobic contributions to the 400 meter dash are higher in women than in men. For example, Duffield et al. (2005) found that men were about 41% aerobic and that women were 45% aerobic. This same pattern has been true in every study I have read: the aerobic percentages are higher in women.

The most obvious and logical explanation is that women take longer to run the 400 meter dash than men, and that is certainly true. The mens world record is 43.03 seconds, and the womens world record is 47.60 seconds, a difference of 4.57 seconds. The difference is even larger at the high school level. The US national high school record for men is 45.19 and 50.74 for women, a difference of 5.55 seconds. Since aerobic contributions increase based on the duration of the event, it makes sense that women use slightly more aerobic energy than men for the 400 meter distance.

Arcelli (1995), as cited in Arcelli et al. (2008), went one step further and studied men and women who ran identical times. In this study, the researcher controlled for the fact that male athletes typically run faster than female athletes for the same 400 meter distance. When Arcelli et al. conducted research on both men and women who ran identical times, they found that women produced higher levels of lactic acid and depended on a higher percentage of aerobic contributions than men did for the same distance and identical time.

Implications

Women and girls rely on higher aerobic contributions for the 400 meter dash than men and boys. As important as the aerobic component is for men, it is even more important for women. We have been mentioning the 60/40 ratio throughout this book, but if you are a high school girls coach, the ratio for aerobic and anaerobic for adolescent girls is probably closer to a true 50/50. While training male and female athletes for the 400 meter dash is going to be largely the same, these findings indicate that you should provide even more aerobic training for your female athletes than your male athletes. The reloading weeks for these athletes should be more like 50/50 than 60/40.

Age Differences

Most of the research studies on aerobic and anaerobic contributions to 400 meter athletes have been conducted on adult male and female athletes. In many cases, these athletes have been highly trained elite athletes. There was one study that was particularly fascinating, because they focused specifically on the differences between children, adolescents, and adult 400 meter runners. The research from Vilmi et al. (2016) is of particular interest to us, since this book is focused on training high school 400 meter runners.

In their conclusion, Vilmi et al. (2016) wrote, "Adult athletes used mainly anaerobic energy and achieved greater acidosis than adolescents and children, who used mainly aerobic energy" (p. 7). This is a significant finding, as it indicates that the 60/40 anaerobic to aerobic ratio that has been widely accepted and publicized is accurate for adults, but that adolescents use much higher than 40% aerobic energy when running a 400 meter race.

Children have lower anaerobic capacity than adults mainly because of hormonal and strength development (Zwiren, 1989). During puberty and throughout the remainder of adolescence, the athlete develops a stronger anaerobic system all the way into adulthood. Vilmi et al. (2016) defined children as 13 and younger, adolescents as 14–16, and adults as 18 and older.

AGE	ANAEROBIC	AEROBIC
Children	39%	61%
Adolescents	45%	55%
Adults	53%	47%

Table 3: As you can see in this table, the younger the athlete the more they rely on aerobic energy for the 400 meter dash.

Vilmi et al. (2016) found that adults relied on 53% anaerobic energy, which is lower than our generally accepted 60 percent. Adolescents, which would be high school aged athletes, relied on only 45% anaerobic energy and children relied on even lower, 39% anaerobic energy. Even if you add several percent to each of these numbers, the researchers found that high school 400 meter runners rely on closer to 50/50 aerobic to anaerobic energy in their event when compared to the 60/40 numbers for adults.

Implications
As a high school coach, the implications of this research are clear, and they perfectly support the thesis of this book. Your 400 meter runners need a balanced approach to training that includes both aerobic and anaerobic training throughout the season. Another major implication is that your younger athletes, particularly your freshmen who are newer to running, should receive a healthy dose of aerobic training. The younger they are, the more you should prioritize aerobic training. In fact, younger high school athletes who are still maturing and developing through puberty are not even physically ready for such heavy amounts of anaerobic work.

Aerobic to Anaerobic Switch

When racing at maximal effort, track athletes rely on a combination of anaerobic and aerobic energy. The two engines work in tandem, not in isolation. As we already noted, Spencer and Gastin (2001) produced a groundbreaking study to show the percentage of aerobic contribution to the 400 meter dash was higher than traditionally thought. They also found that anaerobic and aerobic contributions change dramatically throughout a 400 meter race.

At the beginning of the 400, the athlete relies mostly on anaerobic energy, and later in the race the athlete relies mostly on aerobic energy. They found that the switch from mostly anaerobic to mostly aerobic occurs around 30 seconds into the race. Spencer and Gastin (2001) produced a diagram that captured aerobic and anaerobic contributions at every 10 second segment throughout a 50 second 400 meter dash performance.

Time Segment	% Anaerobic	% Aerobic
10 seconds	80	20
20 seconds	65	35
30 seconds	50	50
40 seconds	42	58
50 seconds	40	60

Table 4: This is a table that I created based on the research of Spencer and Gastin (2001). Early in the race, the athlete depends heavily on anaerobic energy. Throughout the race, they rely more and more on aerobic energy.

The 50/50 Crossing Point

Spencer and Gastin (2001) produced these diagrams for a variety of race distances: 20 seconds, 50 seconds, 110 seconds, and 230 seconds. These durations correlate closely to the 200, 400, 800, and 1500 meters. They found that in every event the athlete relies heavily on anaerobic energy to start the race, which is exactly what we described earlier with the ATP–CP system and anaerobic glycolysis.

The 50/50 crossing point (the point where the athlete is relying equally on aerobic and anaerobic energy) occurs *sooner* as the distance gets *longer*. As we stated above, this occurs around 30 seconds for the 400 meter dash. For an 800, it occurs around 25 seconds. For the 1500, it occurs as early as 15 seconds into the race.

If we apply this research to a high school 400 meter runner who finishes in 60 seconds, they are running *half* the race (from 30–60 seconds) where their bodies are relying more heavily upon their aerobic energy system than their anaerobic system.

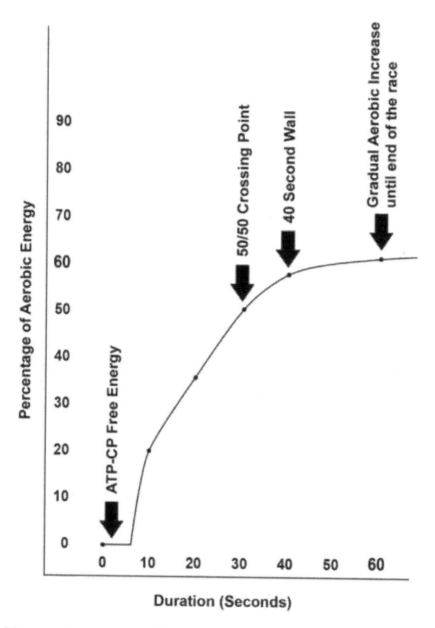

Diagram 3: Throughout the 400 meter dash, the athlete becomes increasingly dependent on aerobic energy to maintain their effort. After 30 seconds, the athlete relies *primarily* on aerobic energy all the way to the finish line.

Athletes Win from Their Strengths

Coach Hart told me multiple times, "athletes win from their strengths." He was referring to the difference between Type A runners (200/400 specialists) and Type B runners (400/800 specialists). I knew from my own experiences as an athlete and coach that he was right, but I wanted to test this concept against scientific research to see if the exercise scientists agreed. I wanted to see if Lab 1 would confirm our Lab 2 theory. I found two studies from the mid-1990s that proved Coach Hart was spot-on accurate.

Weyand et al. (1994) and Nummela and Rusko (1995) both found differences between what they called "sprinter" types and "endurance" athletes. Both studies found that sprinters relied more on their anaerobic strength and endurance athletes relied more on their aerobic strength when racing the 400 meter dash. Weyand found this difference to be 3%. Nummela and Rusko found this difference to be 8%. In other words, when a sprinter and a mid-distance runner both run 50 seconds for the 400 meter dash, they are not using the exact same aerobic and anaerobic contributions. While the general rule of 60/40 still applies, it *may* be as high as 65% anaerobic and 35% aerobic for a sprinter and, conversely, 55% anaerobic and 45% aerobic for a distance runner.

The implications here are clear: short sprinters have a clear advantage in raw speed and their anaerobic system, while mid-distance runners have the clear advantage in aerobic strength and endurance. Neither of these are surprising, since these are the physical skills they have been training toward throughout their running careers. As a coach, you want to continue to develop your athletes' strengths, while working to improve their weaknesses.

You should not train Type A and Type B 400 meter runners exactly the same, but you should be mindful of the strengths that each athlete already possesses and where they need to improve their weaker area. The Type A runner will likely thrive with anaerobic training, but we would caution you not to neglect the aerobic system. The Type B runner already has the aerobic endurance necessary for the 400, but they would certainly benefit from a select number of higher intensity anaerobic workouts. Reinforce the strength, while improving the weakness.

All Sprint Races are Endurance Sprints

The 400 meter dash has often been labeled as an "endurance sprint" event, and we agree fully with that label. Many would consider the 400 to be the only event that would fall into this category, as 100/200 are short sprints and 800 would be a mid-distance event. We actually believe that, within a narrow definition, all sprint races are endurance sprints. Whether it be 100, 200, or 400 meters, athletes are all slowing down in the last part of the race and the event becomes increasingly aerobic the further you run. The best runners in each of these events are those who have the proper training to *decelerate the least* near the end of the race.

Let us consider the 100 meter dash. If you break the 100 meter dash down into 10 meter sections, you will find that world class sprinters usually have their fastest 10 meter section between 50 and 60 meters. They hit top speed around 6 seconds, which we already learned is also when the ATP–CP system is depleted. So what is the goal of the last 40 meters? Slow down less than the other athletes. Nobody is accelerating in the final 10–20 meters. The athletes who win are often those who decelerate the least in the last stages of the race. Duffield et al. (2004) calculated the 100 meter dash to be approximately 20% aerobic for men and 25% for women. Thus, there is a small endurance component even in the 100 meter dash.

This becomes even more obvious in the 200 meter dash. Let us consider and compare the world record performances of Michael Johnson (19.32 seconds, 1996) and Usain Bolt (19.19 seconds, 2009).
Johnson's 100 meter splits were 10.12 + 9.20 = 19.32.
Bolt's 100 meter splits were 9.92 + 9.27 = 19.19.

At first glance, you would think the athletes accelerated in the second half of the 200 meter dash, but that is certainly not true. The time spent accelerating to top speed makes the first 100 meter split time deceptively slower. If you assume that the acceleration required in the first 100 meters adds approximately one second, then their "flying" speeds would be 9.12/9.20 for Johnson and 8.92/9.27 for Bolt. Bolt slowed down by 0.35 seconds from 100 to 200. Johnson slowed down by only .08 seconds.

I do not know the intricacies of Bolt's training during the 2009 season, but since Coach Hart was Johnson's coach in 1996, we know that Johnson was running the training program prescribed in this book. Johnson's +.08 from the first 100 to the second 100 demonstrates incredible strength and conditioning. While Bolt had the advantage in terms of raw speed, Johnson possessed the advantage in endurance. This is precisely why Johnson thrived in the 400 meter dash and Bolt was limited to racing 200 meters and below.

Obviously we know that the 400 meter event requires a greater amount of endurance than either the 100 or 200. Simple math will show you that the initial explosive speed accounts for a small portion of the 400 meter dash. If you are a world-class male athlete, it will be about 13% (6 out of 45 seconds). If you are a high school athlete running 60 seconds for 400 meters, it drops to 10% (6 out of 60 seconds). No matter how fast you run a 400, you only get 6 seconds of free energy and then for the rest of the race you have to rely on how you have trained your body to handle the buildup of lactate that you will inevitably experience late in the race.

We are not saying that you should train 100 meter and 400 meter runners the same. That is the exact opposite of what we would suggest. What we are saying is that athletes slow down in the later stages of every sprint race in outdoor track (100, 200, and 400). This is true of high school athletes just the same as it is for world class runners. The athletes who win these races are those who decelerate the least, those who have the best *race-specific* endurance to finish strong. This race-specific endurance looks different for 100 meter runners and 400 meter runners, but every sprint race requires an endurance component. Thus, we contend that all sprint races are, to some degree, an endurance sprint.

TRAINING TOPICS

This section of the book is a collection of different topics related to the 400 meter dash. These concepts do not fit neatly within the science and physiology section, nor are they specific examples of workouts, but they are important concepts related to coaching the 400.

Runner Types A, B and C

When we think about 400 meter athletes, we can classify them as three types.
Type A is the 200/400 runner.
Type B is the 400/800 runner.
Type C is the very rare runner who can race well at 200, 400, and 800.

If you have a championship level 400 meter runner, that athlete should either: 1) be fast enough to make your 4x100 relay team or 2) have enough endurance to make your 4x800 relay team. Usually it is one or the other, they either naturally possess sprinter's speed or half-miler's endurance. If they cannot do either, they are probably not going to be a great 400 meter runner.

As we have discussed, everyone wins off their strength. One of the mistakes many coaches make is that we spend too much time working on an athlete's weakness instead of developing their strength. When training the Type A runner for the 400, you need to constantly remember that their speed is their best asset. Do not neglect their speed development while you improve their endurance. If you are training Type B athlete, continue to emphasize their endurance and gradually improve their speed. Focus first on their natural assets and then help them improve their natural weakness. Do not forget what brought them success in the first place. Adjust numbers of repetitions or goal times as follows.

How do you Train Types A and B Together?
If you have Type A (200/400) and Type B (400/800) runners, you can train them together but you need to adjust the numbers and cater to the strength of each runner. If you are in mid-season and you are running 200s, you could have the Type A runner do 5 or 6 of them at a specific time and have the Type B runner do 8 to 10 of them at that same pace, or a second or two slower.

Another idea would be to implement the same workout, but have the Type B runner extend the distance of each repetition. For example, you might do 2x450 with the Type A runner but you add a third 450 for the Type B runner. Or if the Type A runner is doing 2x450, you have the Type B runner do 2x550. You could have them run together and you can keep them on the same recovery, but a minor tweak to the number of repetitions and goal times will still allow you to cater to the strength of each type of runner.

In the Mix Once Again

One of the key attributes to success in any endeavor is repeatability. How consistently can you replicate success? The term "one-hit wonder" is generally attributed to a musician who has one major hit song and then falls flat in all future endeavors. We have all observed coaches like this. A coach has one superior talented runner who wins every championship possible, and then they are never able to repeat anything near that level of achievement. These are probably not the coaches you should take advice from.

One of the most compelling aspects of this balanced approach to training 400 meter athletes is the amazing success at every level of track and field. Not only did Coach Hart have four different athletes earn a combined 11 Olympic gold medals, but he also won 20 NCAA Division I championships in the 4x400 meter relay. At one point, his 4x400 relay team earned All-American honors 23 times in a stretch of 26 years. That is the definition of repeatability.

High school coaches who have adopted this program and modified it for younger athletes have also achieved incredible results. When I first adopted this training program in 2008, it had been a while since our school had success in the boys 4x400 meter relay. The last time we had qualified for the state finals was back in 1997, over a decade prior. In our second year implementing this program, we were state runners-up in the 4x400 meter relay (Indiana has a single class with over four hundred high schools competing in the same division). The next year we were state champions. During the several years that I coached, we consistently qualified for the state finals and we regularly developed 400 meter runners to get faster each year. I do not write this to brag about my coaching abilities; rather, I write this to say that I saw firsthand how well this training program worked with our high school athletes. There are numerous other high school coaches across the country who have shared these same types of success stories with Coach Hart, as he has traveled the country speaking at different clinics.

An incredibly talented athlete might have initial success, but they will not continue to improve year after year if they do not develop a proper aerobic base. If you want success over the long haul, if you want to develop an assembly line of fast 400 meter runners and 4x400 relay teams each year, this balanced approach works.

Record Keeping
As Adam Savage, co-creator of the TV show *MythBusters* said, "The only difference between screwing around and science is writing it down." One of the best tools to ensure success and improvement in your training program from year to year is to keep good records of your athletes' workouts, times, recovery, etc. In our observation, distance coaches do this much better than sprint coaches. As a coach, you should keep a book each season and document your training data. There are three major reasons why this is so beneficial.

First, it creates a road map that you can improve from year to year. As you document workout data and compare it to race performances, you know precisely what you can change and improve for next year to make sure your athletes are better prepared. Coach Hart, even after 50+ years of coaching, still made minor changes and improvements each year. He was able to do this precisely because he kept such good records.

Second, it is important for the individual athlete to objectively see their performance data. You can show them what they ran for a similar workout one year prior. You can show them how much they have improved in similar workouts throughout the course of a season. This type of hard data, this objective proof gives the athlete confidence as they prepare for their championship races at the end of the season. The work has been done, now they are ready to perform.

Third, it creates a shadow for athletes to see how they stack up with athletes in the past. For Coach Hart, Jeremy Wariner always wanted to see what Michael Johnson ran for similar workouts several years earlier. Johnson's shadow was left behind at Baylor University within Coach Hart's training logs, and it created motivation for Wariner to chase his predecessor.

Racing the 400: The Four Ps

We recommend breaking up the 400 meter dash into 100 meter increments. For each 100 meters, there is a different focus, and that is what we refer to as the four Ps.

PUSH 0–100 meters
PACE 100–200 meters
POSITION 200–300 meters
POISE (or PRAY) 300–400 meters

Virtually every correctly-run 400 meter race has this same pattern:
First 100 = 3rd fastest split
Second 100 = fastest spit
Third 100 = 2nd fastest split
Final 100 = slowest split
Sometimes, the 2nd and 3rd fastest splits are switched, but the fastest split is always the backstretch and the slowest split is always the homestretch

PUSH
For the first 100 meters, you want the athlete to focus on their start, the first 6 seconds of hard acceleration, and then relax slightly and find their correct race pace before they hit the backstretch. How the athlete runs between 50 and 100 meters is especially important. As we mentioned earlier with the 6 seconds of free energy, we tell the athletes to get out as hard as they can for that first 50 meters, but then they have to settle in at that point.

Let us give an example to illustrate the difference here. Let us say that Runner 1 and Runner 2 are both instructed by their coach to hit 12-flat at 100 meters. Runner 1 follows our approach; they get out hard that first 50 and then slightly relax into their pace. They hit 12 seconds perfectly on the mark at 100 meters and are set up nicely for the second 100. Runner 2 is a little slower to accelerate, so they are a few steps behind Runner 1 as they hit the 50 meter mark. Runner 2 wants to catch up, so they drive a little harder from 50–

100 meters and at 100 meters they are also at 12-flat. Runner 1 has the clear advantage at this point as they have conserved more energy, which they will need desperately on the homestretch.

This first 100 meters is particularly important in the 4x400 meter relay, where so many high school runners drive way too hard between 50–100 meters when they are trying to quickly catch up to their opponent. The inevitable result is that the athlete fades hard on the homestretch, leaving an even larger deficit for their next teammate to try to make up.

PACE

When we talk about trying to run a 400 meter race at a proper pace, we do not mean that each 100 is the same speed. In fact, your first 200 meters should always be faster than your second 200 meters. That is true at all levels, including Olympic finals and world record performances. Coach Hart likes to see a +2 differential for collegiate men and +3 differential for collegiate women. A 46 second male would ideally be 22 / 24 = 46, which would be +2. A 53 second female would be 25 / 28 = 53, which would be +3.

Most high school athletes will be +4, +5, or higher for their 400 meter dash, which means their first 200 meter split is 4–5 seconds faster than their second 200 meter split. This indicates two things: (1) they need to slow down the first 200 and control their race plan on the backstretch and (2) they need to increase their aerobic training to allow them to maintain their speed better on the final homestretch.

If you have run the first 100 meters correctly, you want to be cruising down the backstretch at your proper pace. Again, you want to set a goal time and try to set up a differential somewhere around +3 from the first 200 to the second 200. As a coach, setting up at the 200 meter mark and providing your athlete with a 200 meter split is the most helpful data you can provide them during the race. The 200 meter split is the single most important metric in a 400 meter dash (besides, obviously, the finishing time).

You cannot fool Mother Nature. You cannot overshoot this 200 meter split and expect to hold up in the final stages of the race. The race really begins at the 200 meter mark. The first 200 is just setting up the second half of the race. When 800 meter runners drop down and run the 4x400 meter relay, they are typically very good at hitting this 200 meter split correctly. Then they hold up better than their competitors in the second 200 because of their superior aerobic strength.

POSITION
The second curve, from 200–300 meters, is so important. More races are determined here, tactically speaking, than during any other stage of the race. At this point in the race everyone is slowing down. When it looks like an athlete speeds up here, it is only because the other athletes are slowing down. It is a good rule of thumb that you are going to slow down by at least one second during this 100 meter split, even if you feel you are holding the same pace.

The athlete is also dealing with centrifugal force pulling them to the outside of the track. The athlete does not notice it much in the first 100, but as they start to get tired they feel it more. Athletes can get themselves back into the race or they can really mess up their race plan during this third split. It is a crucial stage in the race.

The athlete does not have a lot of time left nor room for error, but this is where they can make a minor adjustment to set up the final homestretch. If they were a second too quick at the 200, adjust slightly and maintain smooth form through this split. If they were a second too slow at 200 meters, they can focus to increase effort here to make up ground as other runners start slowing down.

POISE (OR PRAY)
We like to say poise here, but sometimes we jokingly say pray. There are only two things that you can put your faith in during this last 100 meters. First, what you have done in training will determine this last 100 meters. Your raw leg speed will not save you if you

have not trained properly for this event. Leg speed is meaningless here, when your muscles are painfully screaming for relief. In most races, that last 50 meters is brutal. You can only expect the body to perform if you have prepared it appropriately. Second, you can trust in your race plan. Everyone is fading in the last 100 meters. Hanon and Gajer (2009) found that, scientifically, the *optimal* 400 meter performance includes a 15% decrease in velocity on the homestretch of the race. Everyone is slowing down, but if you have properly set up your race you can slow down less and, thus, win the race.

A good rule of thumb for a Type A (200/400) runner is that the runner should be about 1–2 seconds slower through their 200 meter split than their 200 PR time. A well-trained 400 meter runner should not slow down more than 2–3 seconds in their second 200 meter split.

Most high school runners run too fast for the first 200 meters. In an effort to prevent this mistake with his athletes, Coach Hart would often walk with his 400 runners over to the 200 meter mark and point out that there are no benches on the backstretch to stop and take a break. If the athlete is going to err, they should go out slightly too slow rather than too fast. They can recover in the second half of the race if they are a tick slow at the 200, but there is no way to correct if they are too fast at the 200. Your athletes need a goal for their 200 meter split, otherwise they do not have a clear plan and chances are they will end up going out too fast through 200 and they will pay for it hard when they hit the 40 second wall.

Perfect Examples

These three athletes were all coached by Coach Hart, so we present these examples of properly run 400 meter races. As you read earlier, the backstretch will almost always be your fastest split, followed by the second curve, the first curve, and then the homestretch will almost always be the slowest split. All three of these races are amazing to watch and I highly recommend watching each of these race videos online.

Example #1: Michael Johnson, 1999 World Record

0–100 meters - 11.05 - 3rd Fastest Split
100–200 meters - 21.22 (10.12) - Fastest Split
200–300 meters - 31.66 (10.44) - 2nd Fastest Split
300–400 meters - 43.18 (11.52) - Slowest Split

Johnson's amazing strength allowed him to run 200 meter splits of 21.22 and 21.96. That +0.74 ratio is phenomenal. According to Coach Hart, Johnson was very confident hitting 200 meter splits in the low-to-mid 21 second range because he knew that he would hold up better than other athletes on the homestretch.

Example #2: Sanya Richards-Ross, 2012 Olympic Finals

After several years training with Coach Hart and after earning a disappointing bronze medal in the 2008 Olympics, Richards-Ross was bound and determined to win the 400 meter gold medal in 2012. This was a stacked field, and some of the competitors were known to go out very aggressively through 200 meters. Coach Hart cautioned Richards-Ross to stay away from running in the low 23s for her split, even though other athletes would be in that range.

Richards-Ross got out hard for the first several seconds and then properly found her pace on the backstretch. She came through the 200 meter split in 23.7, which is exactly where Coach Hart wanted her to be. At that point, she had an athlete on her inside ahead of her and three athletes to her outside for whom she had not yet made up the stagger. She hit the 300 split in 35.8, but she still trailed the athlete to her inside and was virtually even with two other athletes. Richards-Ross finally took the lead with about 40 meters remaining and held on to win a tightly contested race. Her 200 meter splits were 23.70 and 25.85, a difference of +2.15. She won gold because she slowed down less than others in the final homestretch.

Wil London surprised the track world in 2017 when he qualified for the US World Championships team in both the 400 meter dash and 4x400 relay. Two weeks earlier, Wil London finished last place (8th) in the NCAA 400 meter dash finals. Throughout the USATF Championships, he advanced through each round without much room to spare. He was the 10th fastest runner in the prelims, and he grabbed 8th place in the semi-finals, earning him the last spot into the finals.

London found himself situated in lane 1, with the entire field in his view to the outside. Coach Hart wanted London to run 21.5 for his first 200 meters, even though many others in the field would be 21-flat or possibly sub-21. To be on the inside lane and to specifically not try to make up the stagger in the first half of the race was a highly disciplined plan. London was patient and followed his coach's instructions, hitting 21.5 perfectly, but he found himself in the very back of the race, not having made up the stagger on anyone. Through the curve London continued to run strong and by the top of the homestretch he moved up to 6th place. Down the homestretch he passed three more runners. The PA announcer called his name in surprise, "And that is Wil London there on the inside!" as he neared the finish line. London ran 44.47, his lifetime PR and he earned a spot in Worlds in both the 400 meter dash and the 4x400 meter relay. His 200 meter splits were 21.50 and 22.97, which was a +1.47 difference.

A Group of their Own

In many ways, the 400 meter dash is the heart of a high school track team. Often, 400 meter athletes are utility athletes that can also compete well in the 200 meter dash, 300/400 meter hurdles, 800 meter run, and both 4x400 and 4x800 relays. When I was a head track and field coach at the high school level, we never had a great team without a strong 400 meter group.

Most high school teams have two training groups. Group 1 are sprinters and hurdlers and Group 2 are the distance runners. We strongly recommend that the 400 meter runners should be a group of their own. It makes no sense for the 400 meter athlete to be doing the same workouts as the 100 meter sprinters and 110 meter hurdles. Those events are dramatically different from the 400.

Can you imagine a football coach saying that they do not coach their tight ends any differently than the center? After all, both players are offensive linemen. Anyone with any knowledge of football will tell you that the role of the center and the role of the tight end are very different and both positions need specific coaching to fulfill their role. We argue that the same is true with 400 meter athletes. They need specific coaching tailored to their event.

400/800 Interchangeability

One of the secondary benefits of properly training 400 meter runners is that they are far more prepared to run the 800 meter run or a leg on your 4x800 meter relay team. The best 4x400 and 4x800 relay teams that I coached had a combination of Type A (200/400) and Type B (400/800) runners.

In 2010 we were in the mix to win the state championship in the 4x400 meter relay. Within our 400 training group we had a clear top 4 and then a bit of a drop off to #5. We also had a really deep 800 meter group that year. When we had a late season injury to one of the top four guys in our 4x400 meter relay team, instead of calling up a short sprinter we turned to a senior 800 meter runner who had only run a handful of varsity 4x400 races in his career. He was running phenomenal 800 splits, and we trusted him on the 3rd leg of our relay to keep us in the mix. That relay at the state meet was deep—the top six teams finished within 2 seconds of each other. Sure enough, our 800 runner held his end of the bargain and he kept us in the mix, and our anchor got the baton in 2nd place and ran down the leader over the final 50 meters to win the state championship. In that case, we did not go down and look for a 100/200 guy to fill the spot, we trusted in the 800 guy because his training included the key aerobic component that our 100/200 meter runners lacked.

The reverse was true the next year in 2011. We graduated three great 800 runners in 2010 and we were looking to rebuild our 4x800 meter relay team that ran 7:41 and placed 9th in the nation the year before. We still had two really fast 800 runners, but that year we convinced two 400 runners to step up in distance and compete on our 4x800 relay team. We were in contention to win the state title with this mixed group of 400 and 800 runners. We won the indoor state title and we finish 2nd in the outdoor state meet, running 7:42. Our Type A 400 runners split 1:55 (lead-off) and 1:56 (3rd leg) in that race.

When you properly train 400 meter runners with this balanced approach, you can move them up in distance to 4x800 when needed. When you properly train 800 meter runners, you can move them down in distance to the 4x400. My observation is that many coaches look at their athletes as binary. The coach labels each athlete as a sprinter or a distance runner, but 400 runners should be versatile enough to move down to the 200 or up to the 800.

Endurance is the Shortest Path

Coach Hart observed: "The main reason we are seeing more of the sprinter type succeed in the 400 meters today is largely due to the fact that we are able to develop stamina and endurance more effectively than we can increase the sprinting abilities of the middle-distance runner." We have written extensively in this book that endurance is required for 400 success, but the truth of the matter is that athletes with better leg speed have more upside potential in the 400 meter dash.

It is much easier to develop endurance in an athlete than to develop speed. As a coach, you can make sprinters *faster* through speed development training, but you cannot make them *fast*. Most short sprint races are won by the athlete with the most physical talent. Those athletes can thank God and their ancestors for superior genetics. You can certainly train them properly for their distance. You can correct biomechanics. You can convince them to fuel their bodies properly, to dedicate themselves to the sport, and to be mentally tough and prepared for race day. But you cannot change their muscle makeup and provide them with a higher percentage of fast-twitch fibers in their hamstrings.

The good thing about the 400 meter dash is that almost half of the energy demands for the race are aerobic in nature. It is much easier to develop endurance in 400 meter runners than it is to improve their raw speed. This is why training for endurance is the shortest path to success in the 400 meter race. As a coach, you can always improve your athletes' aerobic endurance.

Do more volume by slowing down the pace and taking shorter rest. This is true with all athletes, but particularly important with Type A runners. You can still continue to develop leg speed alongside improving endurance. They are not mutually exclusive. This is precisely what we mean by balanced, you can develop both speed and endurance in your athletes at the same time.

Athletes with superior leg speed do have an advantage in the 400 meter dash, but those athletes lose that advantage if they do not have the proper endurance to carry that speed all the way to the finish line.

Mountain Climbers

All amazing feats of human performance require training. At its most basic definition, we train the body to adapt to increasing loads of work and allow ourselves to recover before introducing a heavier load of work. In exercise science, this is referred to as the overload principle. Mountain climbers know this principle well, and we can learn something from them that provides wisdom in our discussion about 400 meter training.

It is theorized that if a helicopter took someone from sea level and dropped them off on the top of Mount Everest, they would die within 30 minutes because of the extreme environment created at a height of 29,032 feet. When mountain climbers attempt to climb a mountain like Everest or K2, one of the biggest challenges they face is oxygen deficiency. As the climbers increase in altitude, there is less oxygen than their bodies are accustomed to and this thinner air wreaks havoc on the body, particularly the lungs and the brain. Despite this challenge, Edmund Hillary in 1953 and over 6,000 climbers since have conquered Everest. For climbers to achieve this, they must train their bodies to acclimatize to the increase in altitude.

The science behind altitude acclimatization is fairly complex, but here is the simple explanation. At Mount Everest specifically, climbers spend 1–2 months at Everest Base Camp (17,598 feet above sea level) to allow their body time to acclimatize to that level of altitude. When climbers move up from there, they go back and forth between different "camps" at various altitudes. They sometimes climb to higher levels and then go back to a lower level to allow their body time to adapt. It is like the old adage: *two steps forward, one step back*. Usually people say this implying that something is inefficient, that the step back is a bad thing. Mountain climbers know that stepping back before proceeding is an essential part of getting stronger. This cautious, gradual approach allows the body to respond to increasing demands while providing the body time to recover and adapt. Given enough time, their bodies are able to adjust to the altitude, and they can reach the summit.

This is actually a perfect illustration of how to train 400 meter runners. We recommend that their initial base phase be 6–8 weeks, just like Everest base camp. This prepares their body for the more intense work that lies ahead. We also recommend that once you get into the competitive season that you reload every 3rd week, just like climbing up for Camp 2 and then retreating to Camp 1 to give your body time to adapt.

The human body is trainable for many amazing feats, but it must be placed under the right kind of stress to ensure it is able to respond and perform. Whether it be mountain climbing or training for the 400 meter dash: If you do not implement the correct type of stress on the body, you should not expect that it will be able to achieve the major feat.

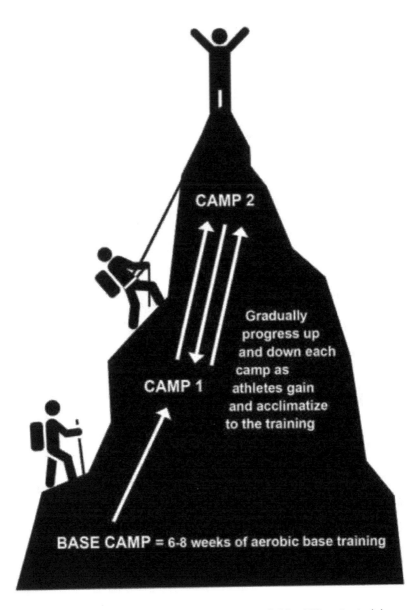

Diagram 4: Mountain climbers provide a great parallel for 400 meter training. After the initial base camp, climbers continue to move up and down the mountain, eventually reaching the peak after their bodies properly acclimatize.

What Goes Down Cannot Come Up

The title of this section is an awkward variation of the old phrase *what goes up must come down*. Because there is a large aerobic component to 400 meter racing, it is relatively easy to "train up and race down" and almost impossible to do the opposite.

The Lesson We Missed in Montreal

At the 1976 Montreal Olympics Alberto Juantorena did something that no man had ever done. Juantorena won both the 400 meter dash and the 800 meter run in the Olympic Games. What most people do not realize is that Juantorena came from an 800/1500 background as a teenager. He was a mid-distance runner, who did not pursue the 400 meter event seriously until his early 20s.

In Montreal, Juantorena first won the 800 meter run. He led most of the race and finished in a world record performance of 1:43.5. He was able to come back a few days later and won the 400 in a time of 44.26. He had developed a great aerobic capacity from his years training as a mid-distance runner and he was able to come down to win the 400 event, as well.

Somehow the coaches of that era missed that lesson. Coaches continued to train with speed, speed, speed—even though the Olympic champion was a former mid-distance runner who won the gold medal based on his endurance. In the 1980s Coach Hart was already moving toward a more balanced approach in training his 400 meter runners, and the lesson to be learned from Juantorena's accomplishment fully landed in his mind. If you have a mid-distance type of runner and you train them primarily as an 800 runner, they will still be able to run a pretty fast 400. That athlete already possesses the combination of aerobic and anaerobic training that they can move down to the 400 fairly seamlessly, just as I found out when I needed a 4x400 relay substitute in a pinch.

If you have a sprinter and you train them primarily as a 400 runner, they will still be able to run a really fast 200 because they are so strong from the aerobic and anaerobic training that they are doing for the 400. Michael Johnson was a great example of this. He broke the world record in the 200 at the 1996 Olympics in the same week where he also won the 400 meter dash. He was training for the 400, but he was also able to drop down and run an amazing 200.

On the other hand, if you are training an athlete primarily as a 100/200 meter runner, it will be very difficult for that athlete to perform a high-quality 400. It is much easier to train up and race down. When you already have aerobic endurance, racing down in distance takes care of itself. If you train for the 800, you can also race down to the 400. If you train for the 400, you can also race down to the 200. If you train exclusively for the 100/200, that is all you will be able to do.

4x400 Meter Relay Thoughts

Selecting the four members of your 4x400 meter relay team is a fairly straightforward proposition. Which four athletes give your team the best opportunity to succeed? Take everything into consideration (health and fitness levels, prior 400 and 4x4 performances, how many other races they will compete in that day, etc.) and select your four runners. Placing them in the correct order to maximize your overall team performance can be a bit more complex.

Lead-Off Leg
The lead-off leg is critical to the success of the relay. Absolutely critical. You want a consistent runner who will not get your team in trouble. This does not have to be your fastest leg, but it should be a highly reliable runner. You cannot afford to have a bad leg at the lead-off position. One school of thought is to put a runner with open 400 experience here, as the lead-off leg is run entirely in lanes. Another idea would be to use an intermediate hurdler or 800 meter runner on this lead-off, as you can trust their endurance to carry them through that final 50 meters without losing crucial seconds before the first handoff.

Leg 2
This is preferably going to be a Type A (200/400) runner. In a 4x400 meter relay, most states run a 3-turn stagger, so you want an athlete that can get out hard and attack the first 6 seconds of that curve to put your team in a good position when everyone hits the break line on the backstretch.

Leg 3
This leg could be anyone, but the key attribute here is a fierce competitor. You want someone who is ready to race no matter what position they are in when they receive the baton. In classic Baylor Bear fashion, Coach Hart calls the third leg a "sic 'em" runner. This needs to be someone who can get your team back into the race and set the anchor up for success.

Anchor Leg

Everything else being equal, your fastest runner is likely going to run the anchor leg. This should be someone with open 400 experience and the ability to close well in the homestretch. While this follows conventional wisdom, there are two examples of when you might want to reconsider.

(1) Do not waste this leg. If you have a sub-par relay overall, sometimes the best way to maximize your runners is to run your fastest leg somewhere in the middle of the relay. This will give your athlete other runners to compete against and it will put you in a better position heading into your anchor leg. It is much easier to run the 4x400 relay near the front of the race than it is trying to catch up the entire time.

(2) If you have two really strong legs. In this case, the second fastest runner may be better suited to be the anchor leg because you can then create a huge mismatch at another leg where your fastest runner destroys the competition. This is obviously a luxury; this would be a very good scenario to have as a coach, as you have multiple elite runners who could serve in the anchor spot.

Assembling the Squad

You do not need four pure 400 meter runners to have a great 4x400 meter relay team. At the high school level you might have two 400 runners, a 200 runner, and an 800m runner or a 300/400 meter hurdler. When you do have multiple athletes with significant experience in the open 400, you have options, particularly at the lead-off and anchor positions. It is not very common for a short sprinter (100/200 type) to make an elite 4x400 relay squad, because they are often not trained properly to handle the aerobic requirements of the event.

Baton Handoffs

There is more time to be gained on a 4x400 relay handoff than in a 4x100 relay handoff. If the athletes get out hard at the start of the exchange zone and exchange the baton somewhere in the middle of the zone, they are keeping the baton moving without losing any time in the handoff. We always set a goal to exchange the baton at the post, right at the finish line (which is half way through the exchange zone). If they are handing off early in the zone, they are losing time in those exchanges because the baton is slowing down as it passes from one runner to the next. Handing off the baton early in the exchange zone often means that the outgoing runner is not up to full speed when receiving the baton. You can shave off half a second per exchange if your athletes do this correctly.

We always recommend exchanging from right hand to left hand. The outgoing runner should be lined up facing the inside of the track, so their left hand would be reaching back to receive the baton. They want to exchange the baton high, at chest/shoulder height and not down by the hips. A good phrase to teach your athletes is to "cherry pick" and keep their arm high. It is difficult for the outgoing runner to reach down to receive the baton. When they reach down, their arms and elbows get jammed up, significantly decreasing mobility. Try it right now: put your left arm straight out (shoulder height) and then move your arm back and forth, toward and away from you. You have much more mobility because your elbow has more range of motion. Now try to reach down as if you were receiving the baton near your hips and try to move your arm back and forth. You get jammed up because your elbow bumps into the side of your body. This is always the job of the outgoing runner. Present their hand high and it forces the incoming runner to exchange it high.

Do Not Test the Runner in Practice

We firmly believe that you should test the runner in competition, not in practice. Practice is always preparation for the real event. The closest thing to testing the runner in practice would be a 320 meter prediction run, but even then we are not truly testing them because with 320 meters they are not even hitting the 40 second wall.

A lot of testing athletes can be done with 4x400 meter relay teams. If you have a 200 meter runner that you want to get a 400 time for, a time trial in practice is not going to provide you with the best data. Put them in a JV 4x400 relay team and let them get a split in an actual race. It sounds simple and many coaches already do this, but there are some coaches who rely on time trial data from practice, and it just simply is not the same thing.

The Multi Event Advantage

When Michael Johnson ran his world-record-shattering time of 19.32 in the Atlanta Olympics 200 meter final, it was his eighth race of the Olympic Games. He is the only man to ever win both the 200 meter and 400 meter events. Back then each event carried an initial first round, a quarterfinal round, a semifinal round, and the final round. Starting in 2004, the Olympics changed to a three-round format for each event. Johnson's balanced training approach allowed him to set an Olympic record in the 400 and then come back a few days later to set a world record in the 200, with numerous races in between.

Different states have different formats for their high school championship track and field meets. Some states have trials and finals on the same day, others have a 2-day format. The 4x400 meter relay is almost universally positioned at the very end of the meet. If you want to coach great 4x400 teams then you need to train them with aerobic endurance to handle multiple high-quality races within a relatively short period of time.

Consider that you have an elite 200/400 meter runner at the state championship meet. Let us assume they qualified in both the 200 and 400 and they were part of your 4x400 relay team, as well. They will have to run multiple rounds of trials and finals throughout the state meet. If they are training on low volume, high intensity, they will probably be overcooked toast after their second or third race. They will run an uninspiring 200 final, and they will be almost worthless at the end of the meet on your 4x400 relay team.

Training your athletes with a balanced approach will allow them to recover better between races and perform better in multiple events. The teams that do this correctly will always find their way to the top of the 4x400 meter podium at the conclusion of the state championship meet.

Championship Week

When you get to your championship week it is better to be under trained than over trained for that week. Assuming that the athlete is in good shape and not coming back from an injury, we want the athlete to come in feeling fresh this week, especially if they have multiple races or rounds of qualifying to deal with. To quote the old phrase: *The hay is in the barn.* If you over train the athlete in the days leading up to their biggest competition, there is no way to correct that and their performance will suffer.

At this point, the athlete is relying on the aerobic endurance they have been building all season to carry them through these final, vital races. When Coach Hart would meet with his assistant coaches the week of a big championship meet, he would ask them to plan out their workouts for that week … and then cut them in half. He would say that tongue in cheek, what he meant was that at this point in the season you have already done all the training necessary for the athlete to run a big performance.

Let us be clear, this is not tapering. We do not recommend decreasing aerobic volume for an extended period of time pointing toward a particular peak date. As you read earlier, we are strong proponents for continual upward movement in fitness levels, supported by reloading weeks. We are recommending that during the championship week your focus as a coach is to get your athlete to the start line feeling fresh and ready to compete.

Don't Fear the Beeper

For many years in the latter part of Coach Hart's career, he relied on an audio beeper device to help guide athletes through their repetition workouts on the track. Coach Hart found and utilized the beeper out of necessity. Early in his career he had very few, sometimes no, assistant coaches to help him run multiple workouts at the same time. He also found that often the athletes were not precise enough in their repetitions and he wanted them to be implementing the workout exactly as prescribed.

Coach Hart found his first beeper device and purchased it for $75 in a pawn shop in 1973. It was a huge metal box and he was able to program it to beep at specific increments. This device allowed him to solve both of these problems with one solution. Over the years, he worked alongside some of his friends who were engineers to develop a better device. Now, coaches can find a variety of these beeper devices to download directly to their smartphone.

One advantage of the beeper is that it forces the athlete to run the entire distance at the correctly prescribed speed. The tendency in short repeats is for the athlete to get out hard, be ahead of their splits early, and then at some point toward the end of the interval they slow down and still hit their final goal time. The athlete mentally knows they were a second or two ahead at the last split, so they are not required to maintain the same exact speed over the final 50–100 meters to still hit their time for that repetition. Of course, this is not a great way to prepare physically or mentally for an actual 400 meter race. The athlete is creating bad habits where they gently fade as they approach the finish line. If they practice this way, chances are they will race this way without even realizing it.

Another advantage is that the coach can program the beeper with different sounds at different time intervals and multiple groups of runners can use the beeper simultaneously to run their workouts. One group of athletes can be running repeat 400s at 64 seconds, and every 8 seconds they will hear a specific noise that will indicate they should be precisely at 50, 100, 150 meters, etc. Another group of athletes can be running repeat 200s at 28 seconds and every 7 seconds they will hear a different noise that will indicate they should be at 50, 100, 150 meters, etc. The athlete should never try to get ahead or behind the beeper, but they should aim to be perfectly even-paced for each repetition.

Coach Hart found that using the beeper allowed him to organize different groups of athletes and workouts at the same time. The beeper also helped the athletes to maintain precise, even splits throughout each repetition for their entire workout.

Strength Equals Speed

A common misconception is that 400 meter training is going to somehow detract from an athlete's 200 meter race performance. All of Coach Hart's athletes ran their best 200 times when they were also in their best 400 shape. If you want to improve your 200 time, you have to get stronger, and training up to the 400 is a great way to improve the strength and endurance you need to run a fast 200.

Strength and speed are synonymous. You will not lose your speed if you maintain your strength. This is true for both aerobic strength and muscular strength. You spend the entire season building up different types of strength in the athlete and then when they experience an injury, illness, or other setback the tendency can be to rush them back to anaerobic training too quickly. Do not forget to reestablish their aerobic strength and muscular strength on their way back to recovery.

If an athlete suffers an injury, a good rule of thumb is 2-to-1: if a runner misses 2 weeks of training it takes them a full week to get them back to where they left off. When an athlete suffers an injury coaches typically treat it with ice initially, followed by heat and physical therapy. Coach Hart would regularly test athletes' hamstring strength at Baylor, and he was able to identify when athletes had previous hamstring injuries because they never properly rehabbed and rebuilt muscle strength after the strain or pull. When one hamstring was far weaker than the other it was clear that the weaker hamstring had previously been injured. To prevent reinjuring that hamstring, coaches need to help the athlete rebuild the strength of that muscle. In addition to balancing strength between hamstrings and quadriceps, you should also work to balance the strength between both left and right hamstrings to prevent another injury.

SPECIFIC TRAINING AND WORKOUTS

At the risk of sounding like Gene Hackman in the movie *Hoosiers* as he measures the basketball rim to be the standard 10 feet above the ground, the 400 meter dash is the same distance everywhere. Whether it be a 14-year old competing in a dual meet in Small Town, USA or a 25-year old professional athlete crouching in their starting blocks at the world championships, the 400 meter dash is the same event.

As a high school coach, training 400 meter athletes is not much different than training college or professional runners. You can run the same repetitions with the same amount of rest. The factors that change are volume (in some cases) and intensity level (in almost all cases). Those are the components of the workout that you need to adapt as a high school coach. Throughout these training sections, we will show you workouts that were implemented with some of the fastest 400 meter runners in world history. We will also provide some specific advice on how to adapt these workouts and concepts for high school athletes.

What is Percentage Training?
As the coach, you carefully analyze your training program and determine what percentage of aerobic work and anaerobic work you are doing each week in your training volume. Classify each aspect of your workout and evaluate the numbers. As you read earlier, we recommend beginning high on the aerobic side, about 10/90 (10% anaerobic and 90% aerobic) at the very beginning of the season and gradually work your way down to 60/40 (60% anaerobic, 40% aerobic) during the competitive phase. We never want to be any higher than 70/30, meaning that we never want to go any lower than 30% aerobic work in a particular week.

Decrease the Rest Time
One of the biggest changes that Coach Hart made over his decades of coaching 400 meter runners was to decrease the amount of rest time that his athletes received between repetitions. What used to

be 15 minutes dropped to 10 minutes later in his career and what would have been 5 minutes in the past dropped to 3 minutes. This decreased rest time was vital to emphasize the aerobic component of workouts later in the season. And, of course, the athlete must go through the aerobic base period and build their oxygen delivery system early so they can handle fast workouts with shorter rest later in the season.

What is a "Swing Down"?

When we refer to swing down, we are referring to a steady deceleration after running at near top speed. We do not want the athlete to immediately slow down; rather, we ask them to coast in their stride, to decrease their arm motion, and to allow themselves to naturally slow down from top speed to a jog. Once you hit the marker that ends the fast sprint, you "swing down" into deceleration until you hit the mark where you finish the repetition.

What is a "Flying" Run?

You will often hear coaches refer to their athletes running "flying 20s" or "flying 30s". They are referring to repetitions at the highest speed an athlete can run for 20 meters or 40 meters, after a short acceleration buildup to top speed.

What is a "Ladder" Workout?

When we mention a ladder workout, we are talking about a workout that has various distances that can increase, decrease, or do both throughout a workout. For example, if the athlete ran distances of 100, 200, 300, and 400 meters that would be an example of an increasing ladder. If the athlete ran 400, 300, 200, 100 meters that would be a decreasing ladder. You could do both, as an athlete might run 100, 200, 300, 200, 100 meters, which would combine increasing and decreasing ladders.

Adjustments Are Essential

You cannot take any training program (this one included) and just implement it exactly as prescribed. You, as the coach, have to be flexible and determine what is most important and when you need to emphasize certain aspects of training. You know which track meets are most important in your schedule. Training athletes for the 400 meter dash is really a series of mini seasons throughout the year and you already know which meets to use to evaluate these mini seasons.

This training program was built on a college schedule where the athletes only race on weekends. One of the biggest challenges for high school coaches is that you have weekday meets and often multiple meets in the same week. As a coach you will have to sacrifice some of your race performances and "train through" those midweek meets. That is really the only way to get in the proper volume of work with your athletes.

Training programs are created in the ideal situation, but you have to be flexible and adjust your plan based on a myriad of factors: meet schedule, athlete's training start date, injuries, weather, etc. You always have to be ready and willing to make adjustments to the plan while sticking to the key principles.

Build a Pyramid, not Pisa
Previously, we used the Egyptian pyramid to visualize what a proper training foundation should look like. Let us take a moment to visualize what it looks like when you ignore the foundation. In northern Italy, along the western coast is a small city with a building that is world renowned. In 1173 construction began in this city to build a tower. Unfortunately, the ground where this tower was located was very soft, and builders did not put down the proper foundation to adjust for the softness of the ground. Within 5 years, the tower started leaning because the foundation was not strong enough. Over the next 200 years various engineers tried to fix the tower with modifications above the ground. They did succeed in stabilizing the building, but they were never able to fully correct the problem. You could visit the famous Leaning Tower of Pisa today, 850 years later, and still see what happens when you do not build the proper foundation.

This is what happens to 400 meter athletes who neglect the aerobic component of the event. The higher the Tower of Pisa was built, the more obvious it became that there was a mistake made at the beginning. Watch a 400 meter race late in the track season, particularly after the 40 second wall, and it will be equally obvious which coaches and athletes neglected their own training foundation months earlier.

Slow Down to Run Faster

We say slow down to run faster. The idea here is that by backing off the pace and not going all out, you can run more volume, more repetitions, and you will be building the perfect balance of aerobic and anaerobic conditioning that it takes to be a great 400 meter runner. This is somewhat of a misnomer, as it implies that all of our training is slow. That is simply not true. We incorporate short, fast sprinting multiple times each week, as you will see in the specific training chapters that follow.

Spikes or No Spikes?

Some coaches have athletes run workouts in spikes. We believe there is a time and place for spiking up during practice, but we would limit how often athletes do this. The three occasions when spikes are appropriate: practicing block starts, simulating race pace relay handoffs, and when running a time trial or predictor run. We generally believe that you should test the runner in competition, not in practice. Therefore, we would caution against athletes wearing spikes too often in practice.

How the Workouts are Presented

I present the workouts exactly the way that Coach Hart designed them for his collegiate and professional 400 meter runners. However, this book is designed for high school coaches, so for each workout I add a section to offer some modifications that you can use to implement these workouts with high school athletes.

Do Not Waste the Warmup

The warmup routine Coach Hart used with his Baylor athletes was tougher than some coaches' full workout. A criticism of the Clyde Hart system for training 400 meter runners is that the athletes are training too much aerobically and not developing their speed. One needs to only look at the warmup and cool down routines to see that speed development is actually taking place during every single practice.

Here is the basic structure of the warmup, with each element listed below in more detail.
- 4 laps of in-and-outs
- Active stretching and drills (no static stretching)
- Accelerations: 4x30–40 meters
- 20/40/60/80 (meters)
- 25/50/100 (meters)

In-and-Outs
For the first part of the warmup, athletes run four laps, alternating between slow and fast running.
For lap 1, athletes will jog 100 meters, then run fast 100, jog 100, run fast 100.
For laps 2 and 3, they do the same thing but the fast 100s should get a little faster each lap.
For lap 4, they jog 200 meters and then run a hard 200.
The athletes are allowed to determine their own speed, but they know that they should be getting faster each lap on the hard segments.

Active Stretching and Drills
We recommend a series of active stretches, not static stretches. Static stretching is like a rubber band: it tightens the muscle during the stretch, and then the muscle goes back to its normal state. It fools the athlete into thinking their muscles are ready for a hard workout. Do not have the athlete do static stretching if they are going to run immediately after. We recommend a variety of active

84

stretches to engage and prepare their muscles for the harder effort. This move from static stretching to active stretching is something else that has come from exercise science research (Lab 1) over the past few decades.

For the drills, we want to engage the leg muscles in dynamic movements. You could use the good old-fashioned high knees, butt kicks, and bounding exercises. A skips, B skips, and C skips are also really good for active drills. A quick online search will help you identify several high-quality active stretches and drills you might incorporate within your warmup routine.

Accelerations

Then we recommend 4 sets of accelerations, somewhere between 30 and 40 meters. You do not necessarily need to hit full speed. Rather, you want to engage your muscles with standing takeoffs where you quickly accelerate for 3–5 seconds. For accelerations, Coach Hart had horizontal lines painted on the track at Baylor so that his athletes could identify the length of each stride as they accelerated out of a standing start. Prior to the lines being painted, he used painter sticks (the kind you use to stir the paint) and he placed them on the track at specific distances.

20/40/60/80 (Meters)

For this, you will need to place cones on the homestretch at 20 meters, 40 meters, 60 meters, and 80 meters. You will have the athletes run 4 sets of 100 meters in this manner.

#1 - Sprint hard to 20 meters, then swing down 80 meters.
#2 - Sprint hard to 40 meters, then swing down 60 meters.
#3 - Sprint hard to 60 meters, then swing down 40 meters.
#4 - Sprint hard to 80 meters, then swing down 20 meters.

25/50/100 (Meters)

For this final part of the warmup, we recommend using a football field.

From 0–25 meters, have the athletes run ½ speed.

From 25–50 meters, have the athletes run ¾ speed.

From 50–100 meters, have the athletes run near full speed.

Set up cones in the end zone and have athletes jog over to the other side and then start again. Have the athletes run these continually for 1–2 minutes.

As you can see, there is a lot of emphasis on speed development incorporated into this warmup routine. This warmup takes about 30–40 minutes, much longer than the workout itself. It is really important the athletes are dialed in and completing this warmup properly, as it serves the dual purpose of preparing them for the main workout (to prevent injury) as well as speed development. Too many coaches and athletes waste the warmup and cool down routine.

Shock the Body in the Warmup

Have your athletes ever run a really hard workout and inexplicably the first repetition of the workout felt the hardest? Often, the second rep somehow feels easier and smoother. This is likely because the warmup routine did not properly signal to the athlete's body that a hard effort was about to take place. A high-quality warmup routine will shock the body awake prior to the workout. The body will adapt, but it has to experience a level of stress before it will be fully prepared. That is part of the reason why we incorporate some really fast running into our warmup routine.

High School Modifications:

The overall volume of this warmup routine is too much for many high school athletes, particularly younger runners. We recommend that you incorporate most or all components but make adjustments to the volume of each. For the in-and-outs, maybe decrease to 2 or 3 laps. It is still important to get your muscles warmed up with some type of running prior to active stretches and drills. For the other 3 components, you could eliminate one and/or drop the overall volume. We do believe that it is important that you incorporate some acceleration work and speed development as part of your warmup routine, but your athletes are likely not ready for the volume and intensity listed above. Create your own warmup routine and stick with it. Be intentional and consistent and monitor this daily to make sure the athletes are doing it correctly.

Cool Down with Speed

During the cool down routine we want to incorporate some speed development, just like we did in our warmup. The difference here is that we want to teach the athletes how to run fast and maintain proper form even when they are tired.

Here is an example of a college cool down routine:
- Wait 10–15 minutes after the workout is finished
- 4x40 yards (20 yards fast, 20 yards swing down)
- 10 more minutes rest
- Then either: (1) 5 minutes jog around the track or (2) 2x30/30s

4x40
We recommend 4x40 yards (on grass) and only give the athletes 20 seconds in between each. This can be pretty challenging after a hard workout. For each of these, we have the athletes run all out for 20 yards and then swing down for 20 yards. This takes less than 2 minutes total, because it is 4x40 yards with only 20 seconds in between each.

Sets of 30/30s
This is quick and simple. The athlete runs 200 meters in 30 seconds, rests for 30 seconds, then runs one final 200 meters in 30 seconds. You measure the sets by how many fast 200s the athlete runs. This takes 90 seconds total.

High School Modifications:
For the 4x40 yards, you could extend the recovery time in between each set, particularly if the athletes just ran a hard anaerobic workout.

For the 30/30s, you can easily adjust the time goals for your athletes. Some of your elite boys can handle 30/30s, but most of your high school athletes will struggle with doing this after a workout. You might call them 35/35s or 40/40s. We still recommend doing two sets, but you can slow down the goal time and adjust the rest to be 1:1 ratio to their running time.

For the 5 minute jog, I would not change that at all. An easy 5 minute jog after a hard workout is a good way for the athlete to reduce their heart rate, help blood circulate through their muscles and get in some easy aerobic volume. Particularly after a really hard sprint workout this will help begin the process of healing any ligaments, fibers, or tendons the athlete may have damaged during that day's training. If you really want to incorporate static stretching, after the cool down would be the appropriate time for that.

The Weekly Microcycle

Once you get past the initial base phase, we recommend settling into a weekly microcycle like the one listed below. You will find specific examples of these workouts and progressions throughout the rest of this training section.

Monday - Tempo Endurance Workout
Tuesday - Overdistance Intervals
Wednesday - Event Day Workout
Thursday - Sharpening Day
Friday - Rest or Pre-Meet Workout
Saturday - Run (or Race)
Sunday - Rest

Each day there is a different focus. Monday and Tuesday are conditioning days. Wednesdays are event days, so those workouts are simulating the demands of a 400 meter race. Thursdays are a sharpening day where we prioritize anaerobic speed development. Early in the season the weekend is for rest, and as the season progresses the weekends become race days.

Workout Classifications

There are five primary types of workouts that your athletes should be doing throughout the entire season: Speed Endurance, Tempo Endurance, Strength Endurance, Aerobic Running, and Event Running. In this chapter, we will briefly introduce each workout classification and provide a few examples so that we have a common vocabulary.

Speed Endurance
We define speed endurance as short full-speed sprints with very short rest. In many cases, the recovery will be active with slow jogging in between each hard run, but never fully stopping. We will dedicate an entire chapter to this category later in this section.

Tempo Endurance
These workouts are interval sessions, where the distance for each set is less than 400 meters. This is a workout that uses shorter intervals and short recovery to build the athlete's aerobic system. The most common example of tempo endurance would be 200 meter repeats with 2:00 rest between each repetition. We dedicate an entire chapter to 200 meter repeats later in this section. Another example would be 6x300 meters with 2:00 rest or a ladder of different short distances between 50 and 350 meters with a walk or slow jog recovery. The overall volume of tempo endurance workouts can range between 2000 to 3200 meters early in the season and decrease down to around 1000 meters late in the season. For example, athletes might start the season running 16x200 meters and by the end of the season be running 5x200 meters.

Strength Endurance
Strength endurance workouts have two main criteria. First, they last longer than 10 seconds in duration. Second, they include some type of resistance that forces increased knee lift and arm motion. Examples of strength endurance would be 6x150 meters uphill or

6x60 stadium steps. These can easily be added after any type of aerobic workout.

Aerobic Running

These workouts are exactly what they sound like. The athlete is doing purely aerobic running. This would include easy jogging or steady state running at a specific, aerobic pace. Overdistance intervals, particularly early in the season when athletes are doing 800–1000 meter repeats, would fit partially into this category of aerobic running.

Event Running

Event running workouts are exactly what they sound like. The coach designs a workout to simulate the 400 meter race experience for the athletes. These workouts are absolutely vital to proper 400 training. Examples of event running workouts include: 350 meter repeats, 450 meter repeats, Event 300s, and Hare and Hound workouts. We will explain each of these workouts in greater detail.

Percentage of Emphasis Chart for Workouts

Early in the season the athlete should be doing generous doses of all types of endurance training. Throughout the season, you will gradually increase speed endurance workouts and sharply increase event running. You will gradually decrease tempo endurance workouts and strength endurance workouts, and you will sharply decrease aerobic running. As you can see from the table, sharply decreasing aerobic running after the initial base phase is the most dramatic percentage change of any workout type.

Type of Workout	Early Season	Mid-Season	Late Season
Speed Endurance	75%	90%	100%
Tempo Endurance	100%	100%	75%
Strength Endurance	100%	85%	70%
Aerobic Running	100%	20%	5–10%
Event Running	25%	90%	100%

Table 5: This is a chart that Coach Hart created to show the emphasis of different workout types during each stage of the season. As you can see, speed endurance increases steadily throughout the season while tempo endurance and strength endurance decrease steadily. Pure aerobic running sharply decreases while event running sharply increases after the initial base phase.

Fall Training Schedule

Any training schedule is an outline, a guideline for the season. There is an almost zero percent chance that your season will go exactly as expected. Flexibility and adjustments are the name of the game. As long as you follow the key principles we outlined at the beginning of the book and you understand what needs to be changed and why, then it is expected that you might need to adjust your plan multiple times during the season.

Aerobic Base Phase
The first 2–3 weeks of the fall training schedule is only 4 days per week and it is all easy running, active stretching, and active drills. We want to put in these weeks of pure aerobic running before we start our fall training schedule. In college this would be September, for high schools this might be November (after fall sports finish).

After those first 2–3 weeks, here is the general weekly outline of the fall base training phase. We will outline each workout in greater detail one at a time in the sections to follow.

Monday - 200 Meter Intervals (I called these "Volume 200s")
Tuesday - Overdistance Intervals (Progress from 2x1000 to 2x450)
Wednesday - Event Day (Event 300s, 350s, 320s, Hare and Hound)
Thursday - Sharpening Day
Friday - Rest
Saturday - Run
Sunday - Rest

Coach Hart would have his athletes complete their training Monday–Thursday each week. For high school athletes, I would recommend spreading these out more throughout the week and providing some rest days in between. You can adjust the days as necessary to fit your schedule, but make sure that each day has a specific purpose. The Monday 200s and Tuesday overdistance intervals are conditioning workouts. You are training the athletes' oxygen delivery system, specific to 400 meter training. The

94

Wednesday workouts are distances related to and simulating the 400 meter race itself. The Thursday workouts are a set of quicker, shorter speed intervals.

Almost every workout that we do takes less than 15 minutes total. If you are taking more than 20 minutes, you are doing something wrong. You are either running too many repetitions or giving the athletes too much rest. The one exception are the Volume 200s when you are still on the high end of the progression.

It takes a solid 6–8 weeks for the athlete to develop the proper aerobic base during this fall training schedule. After that, you are continuing to build the aerobic system as you begin to develop the anaerobic system. Just like a pyramid, a wider base is required to build a higher pyramid. That same principle is true in 400 meter training.

What to Prioritize
If you are limited on the number of days that you can work with your athletes in the offseason, I suggest prioritizing the two conditioning days (Monday and Tuesday) to be most important and then event day workouts to be third. When I was coaching high school 400 meter runners, we only met three times per week (Monday, Wednesday, and Friday) from November to January and we prioritized workouts in this order.

Cross Country Season
I was a cross country coach who also coached 400/800 meter runners in track. If a 400 runner was not in a fall sport, we would incorporate them into our cross country training. It was actually rather easy. If our cross country team ran 6x1000 meters, we would have the 400 runners do 2x1000. If our cross country team ran a 4–5 mile tempo, our 400 meter runners would do 1–2 miles. It was pretty easy for us to include our 400 meter athletes into our cross country training and they were in great shape when track started in the winter. Most of them never ran a 5k race in cross country. We were preparing them for track season, not for cross country.

With 400 meter runners, I regularly incorporated speed endurance training throughout the entire cross country season. That is when the 400 athletes would be completely separate from the cross country runners. Sprinters should be practicing fast running at all stages of the year-long training plan. Aerobic conditioning is the primary focus in the early stages of training, but that does not mean that you cannot incorporate fast running. If you look back at the table in the Workout Classifications chapter you will see that speed endurance workouts are incorporated throughout every phase of training.

What About Late Starters?
The high school sports schedule is much different from the collegiate season. Coaches often ask: If an athlete is a multi-sport athlete, how do you train them for the 400 meter dash? The answer is simple: You adjust their overall training schedule, but you still have to get in at least 6 weeks of the aerobic base training as soon as they begin their track season. You can modify many things as a coach, but you cannot just drop them into the training cycle with everyone else.

If you have them jump right into heavy anaerobic training, you should expect that they will run their fastest races early but their ceiling is lower and they are more likely to stagnate late in the season. We realize this means that you might have to sacrifice a couple of your early meets and the athlete might be impatient. That is where you as the coach teach the core principles of the training plan and explain that they are being prepared to run their best races at the end of the season.

200 Meter Repeats

One of the key workouts through all phases of training are 200 meter repeats with 2 minutes rest in between each repetition. This is our favorite Tempo Endurance workout during the base phase. When I was coaching we called this workout "Volume 200s" early in the season. I wanted the name itself to describe to the athletes what we were trying to accomplish.

Here are the key components to this workout:
1. You start with a high volume of 200s and then gradually you decrease the volume each time that you run this workout.
2. Each time you do this workout, the athlete should aim to improve their overall average (by roughly a second).
3. The conditioning comes primarily from the short rest period, not in the speed of the running itself.
4. This is not racing, you do not want the athletes to be trying to run way faster than their prescribed goal time.

For week 1 with collegiate runners, Coach Hart would start the men at 16x200 @ 36 seconds and the women at 16x200 @ 40 seconds. Each week they would drop one repetition and try to run one second faster. Here is what that progression looked like for Coach Hart:
Week 1 - 16x200 @ 36 (men), 40 (women)
Week 2 - 15x200 @ 35 (men), 39 (women)
Week 3 - 14x200 @ 34 (men), 38 (women)
Week 4 - 13x200 @ 33 (men), 37 (women)
Week 5 - 12x200 @ 32 (men), 36 (women)
Week 6 - 11x200 @ 31 (men), 35 (women)
Week 7 - 10x200 @ 30 (men), 34 (women)
Week 8 - 9x200 @ 29 (men), 33 (women)

All of these sessions were run on grass. Once they got down to 8x200 (in week 9) they left the grass and went to the track.
Week 9 - 8x200 @ 28 (men), 32 (women)
Week 10 - 7x200 @ 27 (men), 31 (women)
Week 11 - 6x200 @ 26 (men), 30 (women)

Once you get to 6x200 in week 11 that is the magic number. Anything below that becomes anaerobic speed work. In Coach Hart's mind anyone who could run 5x200 @ 25 with 2:00 rest was an elite level athlete. It is a very difficult workout to run that fast for 5 repetitions with only 2 minutes rest.

One might ask: If the athlete can already run 6x200 @ 26, then why do you need to start at 16 and work down? The answer is simple: It is all about aerobic conditioning. If the athletes start at 6x200 then they miss the entire foundation of volume from prior workouts.

Endless Relay Variation:
If you are doing 5x200 and you have athletes running around 30 seconds, then you could implement a 5-person "endless relay" concept. Some people call this Australian Chase. In this variation, the athletes do not run together; rather, they run one at a time and their rest period is while the other 4 athletes are running. You want to do this on the track. To begin, runners 1, 3, and 5 will be positioned at the start/finish line and runners 2 and 4 will be positioned at the 200 meter mark on the backstretch. Runner 1 begins and runs 200 meters in 30 seconds, then runner 2 takes his turn, runner 3, runner 4, and then runner 5. Runner 5 will finish on the backstretch (where Runner 1 is currently waiting) and then you begin round 2. This is essentially a 200 meter repeat workout with 2:00 rest, except the runners are doing it solo instead of as a group. Another variation to support your 4x400 relay would be to add a baton and have athletes practice baton exchanges during each transition.

High School Modifications:
There is no question that there is a wider range of speed and talent in a high school program, compared to a major Division I college team. In a major college team, your best 400 meter runner is probably only about 3–5 seconds faster than your slowest runner. Anyone slower than that would not justify a spot on the roster. However, when I coached high school I would have my fastest boys running 47–48 seconds but I would also have JV runners slower

than 60 seconds. This difference would be even greater if you coach both boys and girls 400 meter runners. As long as the athletes were willing to put in the work, I never cut athletes based on ability level. This does create a challenge for the high school coach with this specific workout.

The obvious answer is that you create different groups of athletes, based on ability level. Our older, varsity boys would run 16x200 with 2:00 rest, but our newer or younger boys might only start with 10 to 12 sets. Then you work the progression the same. The varsity boys would work down from 16, the younger group would work down from 10–12. Keep the rest the same at 2:00 and set appropriate goal times for each runner. A younger boy or girl might have to start at 12x200 @ 40–45 seconds and then progress down from there. 16 is not a magic number–that is just the number that Coach Hart identified for his athletes to get the work accomplished. On the other hand, if you start with fewer than 10 sets then you do not have enough room to progress down the way these workouts are designed.

Remember, the goal of this workout for the first several weeks is aerobic conditioning. The athlete does not have to be running fast times at the beginning of this progression. The whole purpose is to build aerobic endurance, progress down in repetitions over time, and get faster throughout these sessions.

Overdistance Intervals

For the overdistance intervals, we follow a similar philosophy in progression as we do for the Volume 200s. We start with the highest volume and slowest pace at the beginning. Each week we drop the volume and increase the pace. At the beginning of the season, we follow a 5-week progression:

Week 1 - 2x1000 meters, 10:00 rest
Week 2 - 2x900 meters, 10:00 rest
Week 3 - 2x800 meters, 10:00 rest
Week 4 - 2x700 meters, 10:00 rest
Week 5 - 2x600 meters, 10:00 rest

The most important split to give the athlete is what time they should hit for 400 meters. After all, these are 400 meter runners. The 400 meter mark is a split they can understand how to pace correctly. Rather than provide a final goal time, give the athletes a 400 meter split and then tell them to maintain that same speed for the rest of the way. Each week, as you drop 100 meters, you also knock off two seconds from that 400 meter split.

Example:
2x1000 - 400 meter goal time: 80 - (3:20 for 1000)
2x900 - 400 meter goal time: 78 - (2:55 for 900)
2x800 - 400 meter goal time: 76 - (2:32 for 800)
2x700 - 400 meter goal time: 74 - (2:10 for 700)
2x600 - 400 meter goal time: 72 - (1:48 for 600)

During this 5-week progression, the athlete is rewarded. We decrease the distance and slightly increase the intensity. We are not trying to create distance runners—and any distance coach or athlete will assure you that 2x1000 is not a real workout for serious distance runners.

After these 5 workout sessions we are ready to move to the track and continue decreasing volume. Once we hit the track, we follow the same progression, but the last three moves are only 50 meters at a time. Once you are into this second progression (550s, 500s, 450s) you should be approaching your first competitions.

2x550 meters - 10:00 rest - 70 seconds through 400 (96 for 550)
2x500 meters - 10:00 rest - 68 seconds through 400 (85 for 500)
2x450 meters - 10:00 rest - 66 seconds through 400 (74 for 450)

What we outline here is an 8-week progression, though this will often be interrupted by winter break at both high schools and universities. Once we hit 2x450, we do not move back up. Once we start racing, 450 meters is the longest interval that we recommend the athletes run. The only exception is if an athlete gets injured and we need to bring them back into fitness. To prevent re-injury, we would bring the athlete back in at a higher volume and then work them back down to 450 again.

High School Modifications:
You may think that 1000 meter repeats with high school 400 meter runners is a lot to ask, and I agree with you. Most of the 400 runners that I coached were not cross country runners, so it was difficult for them to maintain that proper pace for 3+ minutes. Here is the progression that I used when I coached high school athletes:
2x800 - two weeks in a row
2x700 - two weeks in a row
2x600 - once
2x550 - once
2x500 - once
2x450

As you can see, the volume started at 1600 meters (2x800) instead of the 2000 meters for college runners (2x1000). When you get to 2x450 that is the end of the progression.

Another suggested modification when you get down to 600 and lower is to run a specific pace for 400 meters and then pick it up at that point until the finish. For example, when you run 2x600, run the 400 at a specific pace and then pick it up the last 200 meters. You can do the same thing with 550s, 500s, and 450s. Run a specific pace through 400 meters and then pick it up faster until the finish.

Another modification would be to incorporate two different distances. Instead of 2x700, you might run 1x700, 1x600. This does not significantly change the workout, but mentally it is easier for the athlete if they know the second repetition is shorter.

450 Meter Repeats

As you just read in the section on overdistance intervals, 2x450 meters was the final workout in that progression. At this point, the athletes will continue to run 2x450 meters each week, but they will progress in speed over the next several weeks. We recommend staying with 10 minutes rest in between each set. Years ago, Coach Hart gave his athletes 15 minutes rest in between this workout, but he found that was too much recovery time.

The 450 meter repeats are the culmination of the overdistance intervals, and from the mid-season point to the end of the track season these are the longest intervals the athletes will run. It is important to continue to maintain this one workout per week where the athlete is running further than the race distance. This is just as much mental as it is physical.

What Pace Should These Be?
As athletes run this workout each week, they should get faster. Eventually, you want the athletes to be able to run these within about 5 seconds of their 400 meter race pace. If an athlete can run 50 seconds for a 400 meter race, you want them to eventually be able to run 2x450 in about 62 seconds, coming through 55 seconds at 400 meters. For a 60 second 400 meter runner, they would be running around 73 seconds, coming through in 65 seconds through the 400. Based on their 450 meter goal time, set goal times and record athletes through 200, 300, 400, and 450 meters. One key component is that you want set 1 and set 2 to be nearly identical. You do not want an athlete running slower on the second set. We never want to teach athletes to slow down throughout a workout.

The Surprise Variation
Every once in a while, you can drop this workout down to 1x450 and just let the runners get after it. We recommend doing this before a really big meet, whether in the reloading week before the meet or just in backing off volume the week of the meet. The psychological effect for athletes when they think they will be doing 2x450 and then

you cut it down to 1x450 can be very motivating. Let athletes know right before practice that you are dropping it to one. They end up absolutely flying through the 450, often running near their actual 400 meter race pace. However, this should only be done on rare occasions. Overall, 2x450 is the better workout and you do not want to train your athletes into thinking that you are going to consistently surprise them and decrease workout volumes.

High School Modifications:
We do not recommend any modifications for high school athletes with this workout. You would only adjust the goal times, based on the athlete's current 400 meter race times.

Why 350s Are Magic

Intervals of 350 meters are the perfect distance for college men because of that distance's connection to the 40 second wall. Remember that once you get beyond 40 seconds of near-maximal running, your body's anaerobic system cannot keep up with the energy your body is requiring and your blood lactate levels rapidly increase.

If you ask elite college men to run 300 meter intervals, they will finish each repetition under 40 seconds and they will experience limited lactate buildup throughout the workout, even if they do several sets. On the other hand, if you ask a college male to run 350 meter intervals, they will be running beyond 40 seconds on each and every repetition. Having the athletes practice running hard beyond 40 seconds is the key here.

If your training program does not incorporate hard running sessions beyond 40 seconds, then you are missing this vital component in training 400 meter runners. You are not teaching the athlete to adapt to what will occur on the homestretch in the race. You must replicate for the athlete what they will encounter on race day.

Not all 40 second segments are created equally. For this workout to provide maximum benefit, you must be chasing near-maximum speeds for each set. If you are running a few seconds too slow on each set, you will get very little benefit from this workout. One of the keys to this workout is to run really fast, but "controlled" for the first 200 meters. You want to teach the athlete how to hit the right split at 200 meters, which we have already mentioned is vital in 400 meter racing. You also want to make sure the athlete does not run too fast on the first and second sets and then not be able to hit pace for the third set.

350s Are Not Magic for Everyone
Many athletes will be able to run 3x350 and average pretty close to their 400 meter race time (maybe even a second or two faster). As

we mentioned above, this is a great workout for college men who are running in the mid-40s for 400 meters. However, 350s will be too long for most high school runners.

High School Modifications:
We recommend adjusting the distance so that athletes are running approximately 45 seconds on each set. This might be 300 meters for high school girls or 325 meters for high school boys. For your slower, younger runners this will be less than 300 meters. 350s are the magic number for elite men, but 45 seconds is really the magic number. The 40 second wall applies without discrimination. A world class sprinter or a high school freshman brand new to the 400 will both face their own humanity at the 40 second wall. We recommend that you keep the rest time in between these 350s to no more than 5 minutes. We also recommend capping it at 3x350. If you try to run 4 or more then you start to lose the quality and the athletes will not be able to hold the fast pace needed to accomplish the workout.

If you have athletes across a wide range of ability levels (which many high school coaches do) here is another thought. Reverse the workout. Instead of running 3x350 at a specific goal time, ask them to run 3x45 seconds and set their goal as a specific distance for them to cover. Set up cones every 10 meters, starting at 250 meters and going to 350 meters. For your fastest boys, you might tell them to get to 350 meters in 45 seconds. For another group, you might tell them to get to 300 meters in 45 seconds. This is essentially the same workout, but you are reversing the structure to set the goal of distance covered. But here is the major drawback that you need to adjust for with this design. The athlete still needs specific goal times and splits for each 100 meters. You should not ask them to go "all out" without any data points. If you do that, they will sprint all out the first 150 meters and then slow down for the rest of each repetition, and that is exactly the opposite of how you want them to race. Give them even splits. If you want the athletes to hit 320 meters in 45 seconds, tell them to hit 14, 28, and 42 at each 100 meter split. Do not leave this workout too wide open.

Event 300s

For "event day" workouts we are trying to replicate the physical and mental demands of a 400 meter race. We want to teach our athletes how to race the 400 within practice simulations. Event 300s are a perfect example of how we can achieve this. When I used these workouts, we called them Split 400s.

You already read about the 4 Ps of racing the 400: Push, Pace, Position, Poise. This particular workout emphasizes each of these Ps. Here is the basic structure of the workout:
3 sets of 300 meters fast, rest 1 minute, 100 meters fast
5:00 rest in between sets

For this workout, we want the first 200 of each set to be steady and then we want to speed up through the curve from 200 to 300 meters. The key is to hit a specific "pace" at 200 and then demonstrate "position" to 300. In a race, the athletes often feel like they are speeding up between 200 and 300 meters as they approach the homestretch, but in reality they are slowing down through that curve. In this workout we are specifically teaching the athlete position, to speed up through that part of the workout. Teach the runners to utilize their arm movements to increase their turnover rate.

Goal times for a college male:
300 meters in 40 seconds with 100 meter splits: 14 at 100, 28 at 200, 40 at 300
As you can see, the athlete runs splits of 14, 14, and 12. We are asking them to hit a specific pace at 200 meters and then pick up their speed from 200 to 300 meters.
The 100 meter dash after the 1:00 rest is a hard sprint. That is where you emphasize poise, running fast and emphasizing proper form down the homestretch.

Race Simulation Ideas

We always do this workout starting at the start/finish line to simulate the 400 meter race. This workout is great for the physical demands as well as the mental aspect of how to race properly. We also practice getting out hard in the first 50 meters and then settling in to the proper pace, practicing Push, the first of the 4 Ps in how to race the 400. These are called *Event 300s* for a reason: we are simulating the event itself.

Running this workout (and other event day workouts) in different lanes is another good way to simulate the race. Most of the time, coaches run workouts in lane 1. It is more convenient because the coach and athlete know intuitively where the different marks are on their home track. However, in a 400 meter race the athlete will rarely be in lane 1. They need to practice in lane 4 or lane 8. They need to know how it feels to run in the outside lanes and where the splits are in those lanes.

High School Modifications:

I would not recommend changing much for high school athletes. You want this workout to be high quality and correctly paced, so you might have your younger athletes do only 2 sets. It will be better for them to do 2 sets correctly than to do 3 sets incorrectly.

Another idea for younger or slower athletes would be to have them do the same workout, but cut it down to 250 meters hard, 1:00 rest, 50 meter hard. You will want to implement the same approach, where you give them even splits for 100 and 200 meters and then have them pick up the pace from 200 to 250 meters. You still want to teach them to pick it up on the curve after they come through 200 meters.

Another variation for younger runners would be 3x300 meters, with very specific pace changes. For this workout, the athlete practices running all out for the first 50 meters (to simulate starting a race), then they relax and "float" from 50 to 200 meters. Once they hit 200 meters, then they run all out for the last 100 meters. This is another way to simulate the race for the first 50 meters and the need to pick up effort from 200 to 300 meters.

320 Meter Predictor Run

Every once in a while we suggest doing a 320 meter predictor run. On this day, the athletes only run one set of 320 meters, and you tell the athletes to run it as fast as they can. It is essentially a time trial that you can convert to predict 400 meter performance at different points in the season. We use this very rarely, though, because as we mentioned earlier we believe that you should test the runner in competition, not in practice. You will never have an athlete run the same effort in the 400 during practice as they would in a race.

Here is the formula:
320 meters is equivalent to 350 yards.
Take the athlete's performance from this predictor run and add:
12 seconds for boys or men during the early season
11 seconds for boys or men at mid-season
10 seconds for boys or men late season

For girls or women, add another 3 seconds.
Take the athlete's performance from this predictor run and add:
15 seconds for girls or women during the early season
14 seconds for girls or women at mid-season
13 seconds for girls or women late season

Examples:
If a male athlete runs 35 seconds for a 320 in the early season, he is probably in 47 second shape for a 400 meter race.
If a female athlete runs 45 seconds for a 320 in the mid-season, she is probably in 59 second shape for a 400 meter race.

To give proper credit, Coach Hart learned about this predictor run and formula from Coach Oliver Jackson. Jackson coached at Abilene Christian University from 1948–1963, has been inducted into multiple Halls of Fame, and he coached athletes to 4 Olympic gold medals, 17 American records, and 15 national collegiate records (USTFCCCA.org).

High School Modifications:

These conversions were created for college athletes. For high school conversions, you might need to add a second or two to each category to find the proper conversion rate. Honestly, though, we recommend you only do this a couple times per year at maximum. The high school season is so much shorter than the college season that you typically do not go very long in between track meets. As we mentioned earlier, test the runners in competition, not in practice.

Hare and Hound

This is a fun workout that athletes really seem to enjoy. We do this workout for its physical benefit, but it is also a great simulation for your 4x400 relay running as it teaches the athletes to gradually close the gap on the runner in front of them.

For this workout, we recommend 4x300 with 5:00 rest. This might seem like it contradicts with our love for 350 meter repeats, but 300 is a good distance for this particular workout because (1) you are running four sets and (2) because on 2 of the 4 you are specifically chasing your partner runner. You will still get some benefit of lactate buildup by the end of the workout.

Here is how it works. We start everyone at the 100 meter mark at the start of the backstretch (300 meters from the finish line). You set up two athletes of similar ability level. On set 1, Runner 1 will be the Hare and Runner 2 will be the Hound. The hare starts first and their job is to run a perfectly steady 300 meters (for example: 18+18+18 = 54). The hare takes off and once they hit 15 meters (marked by a small cone on the track) then the hound takes off to chase them.

The hare is only worried about running even splits: 18, 18, and 18. They are not at all concerned with what the hound is doing behind them. The hound's goal is to gradually catch the hare somewhere on the homestretch. Once the hound catches the hare, they maintain that same pace and finish together through 300 meters. The hound has specific instructions not to catch the hare right away, but to spread it out over the entire distance and pull even with the hare on the homestretch.

This is a perfect simulation for how you want to teach your 4x400 runners (legs 2, 3, and 4) to compete if running from behind on their leg of the relay. For set 2, you switch roles. Runner 2 becomes the hare and Runner 1 becomes the hound. Since you are doing 4 sets, each runner assumes each role 2 times.

High School Modifications:
With many high school 400 runners, the only thing you need to modify here would be their goal times for this workout. You can easily vary this workout for younger, slower runners. If you want the runners to run faster, you could drop this down as low as 250 meters to ensure that they run it hard enough. If you want to get more of that 40 second benefit, you could increase up to 320 meters.

Pro tip: You want to keep the athlete from "cheating" and catching up too fast, otherwise they are defeating the purpose of the workout and they will be inclined to go out too hard in their 4x400 relay leg. Establish this rule: If you catch your hare too quickly, you have to pass them immediately and keep running at that same pace. You cannot catch them within the first 100 meters and then just sit on their hip the rest of the rep. This will encourage the hound to catch the hare gradually over the full distance.

30/30s

Most of the time we incorporate these 30/30s into our cool down routine, as you read previously. Sometimes, though, we like to use 30/30s as a stand-alone workout. Again, the 30/30s is simply running a 200 in 30 seconds and then resting for 30 seconds. That would be 1 repetition of 30/30s.

When we get to the competitive season, we like 30/30s as an occasional tempo endurance workout to replace our 200 meter repeats. This workout is especially valuable in reloading weeks during the competitive season as it is a great way to incorporate a strong aerobic component into a speed workout. The pace is not blazing fast, but with only 30 seconds rest this is a workout that incorporates a high dose of endurance.

If you are using this as a workout, we suggest doing 3 sets of 3x30/30s. Set 1 would take 2 ½ minutes, 30 seconds to run 200, 30 seconds rest, 30 seconds to run 200, 30 seconds rest, and 30 seconds to run 200. We recommend taking 3:00 in between each set and we recommend running 3 sets total.

We also recommend this for a workout in sub-par, cold conditions. For one reason, it is short in duration so you can get back inside quickly. For a second reason, you are not asking your athletes to run too fast in cold conditions, so you are protecting their muscles from injury.

High School Modifications:
We recommend dialing back both numbers, but keeping the run-to-rest time the same, with a 1:1 ratio. We recommend their goal time be roughly 2/3 of their 400 race ability.
- So a 45 second runner would be able to handle 30/30s.
- A 50 second runner would be 32–33.
- A 55 second runner would be 36–37
- A 60 second runner would be 40.

If a 60 second runner is running 40 seconds for 200, then they would also get 40 seconds rest. So they would be running 40/40s, with everything else remaining the same.

For younger athletes, you might also dial back the volume. Instead of doing 3 sets of 3x30/30, you might do 2 sets of 3x30/30. Another variation would be to do 3 sets of 2x30/30. You can adjust any of the variables to fit the needs of your runners. The one thing you do not want to change is the 1:1 ratio of running time to recovery time.

Speed Endurance

One of Coach Hart's biggest changes late in his coaching career was increasing the amount of speed endurance drills into his training program. In the last stages of his career, he was doing more speed endurance and acceleration work than ever before.

Speed Endurance
As we mentioned earlier, we define speed endurance as short full-speed sprints with very short rest. In most cases, the recovery will be active with slow jogging in between each repetition without ever fully stopping.

Speed Makers
One of Coach Hart's favorite speed endurance workouts is something he called speed makers. This workout is great to run on a football field, using yard markers. If your high school is fortunate enough to have an all-purpose field, that is perfect. If your school is not in that position, you can still run the same workout and just measure out cones on the grass.

This workout is easier to see visually than it is to read about, so in addition to the explanation we will offer here, you can also look at the diagram to see how this looks on the field.

The athlete should run hard as soon as they pass the goal line. This is not a buildup, this is an explosive takeoff as if the starter's pistol just went off. The athlete accelerates hard and they run at top speed until they hit 60 yards, then they swing down for 40 yards until they get to the opposite goal line.

You will have a cone set up directly in front of the field goal post in the back center of the end zone. Athletes will jog around that cone and then head to the other side of the football field. When we say jog, we mean they can go pretty slow on this segment. In fact, we sometimes say "pitter pat" is the pace they run when they are in the end zone jogging to the next set. It can be a very slow jog, which is perfectly fine.

Once they hit the goal line, they start it again on the other side of the field. The athlete explodes hard and holds top speed until 60 yards, then they swing down for 40 yards. When the athlete finishes 2 loops (4 straightaways), that is one set. We recommend running 2 sets total with a 5:00 break in between.

High School Modifications:
There are ways you could alter this workout. If you want to dial down the rigor, you could go 60/40 on one side and 50/50 or 40/60 on the other side. This would decrease the hard portions and increase the swing downs.

Progressives
One of Coach Hart's favorite adaptations to the speed maker workout is something he calls progressives. On one side of the football field you set up cones at 60 yards and 80 yards and on the other side you set up cones at 70 yards and 90 yards. So one full set of progressives would be: 60/40, 70/30, 80/20, 90/10. This is a much more challenging workout because you are increasing your hard segments and decreasing your swing down segments throughout each set.

The key here is to teach them how to run fast while they are tired, as the recovery is not enough for them to ever get their heart rate back down very far. This combination of speed and strength is exactly what the 400 meter race distance will demand of them.

100s on the Track
Another good example of a speed endurance workout is utilizing the homestretch of your track. Measure and put down cones at 25, 50, and 100 meters in an outside lane. Measure and put a cone down 15 meters past the finish line in the middle of the track. Then measure and put down cones at 25, 50, and 100 meters in an inside lane coming back toward where you started.

The general idea of this workout is to run 3/4 speed to the 25 meter mark, then accelerate to full speed by the 50 meter mark, and then hold top speed to 100 meters. Once the athletes pass the finish line, they should "swing down" and turn around at the cone marked out 15 meters past the line. Then turn around at that cone and head toward an inside lane and repeat the 25/50/100 meters the opposite direction.

There are two variations to this workout: 1 minute and 2 minutes total.
For the 1 minute workout, athletes should get in 3x100 meters. Take 5 minutes rest and then do a second set.
For the 2 minute workout, athletes should get in 5x100 meters. When you do the 2 minute variation, it can be hard for athletes to do a second set. You might just stop at one set, as this is a very tough drill.

High School Modifications:
For the progressives workout, you could decrease the length of the hard segment and still accomplish the same basic concept. Instead of starting at 60 hard, 40 swing down, you could finish at 60/40. Start at 30 hard, 70 swing down and work up from there. One full set would be: 30/70, 40/60, 50/50, 60/40.

For the 100s on the track, you could manipulate any of the distances to decrease the total volume. You could do 75 meters instead of 100 meters. Run the first 25 meters at 3/4 pace, accelerate to top speed between 25 and 50 meters, and then hold top pace from 50 meters to 75 meters.

As we mentioned earlier, the purpose of speed endurance is to practice running at top speed for short bursts with active recovery in between. You can modify any of these workouts to decrease volume and rigor and then they would be perfectly appropriate for high school athletes.

Speed Makers

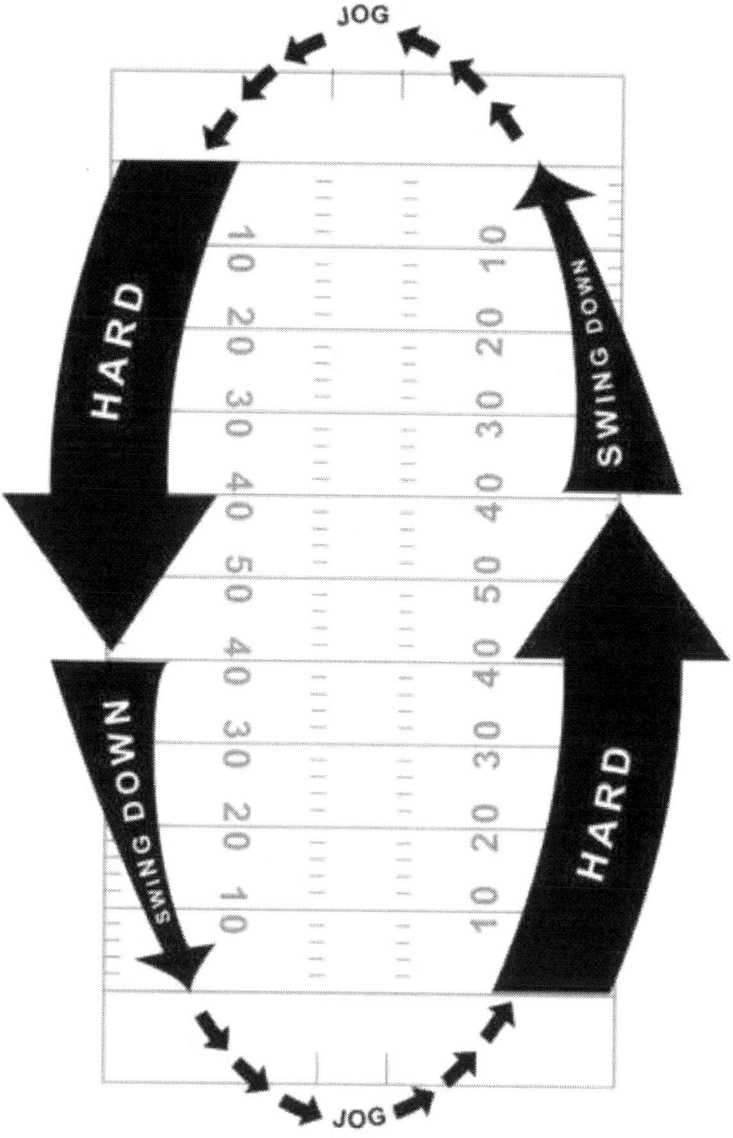

Diagram 5: This is a visual graphic of Speed Makers, where athletes run hard for 60 yards, swing down for 40 yards, and then jog through the end zone to the other side of the field. Two of these loops equal one set of Speed Makers.

Your Pre-Race Plan

We already highlighted earlier in this section the importance of a high quality warmup routine. During practice sessions, the coach can watch this routine to make sure athletes are doing it properly. On meet day, the coach will be busy with a dozen other things, and it is easy to just assume your athletes are warming up properly. If you have amazing, mature, disciplined athletes, then you can rest assured that they will be ready when they toe the line. But since we are writing a book to high school coaches who know that this is not always the case, we recommend that you provide additional structure to the athlete's pre-race plan.

A good pre-race plan will ensure that your athletes are ready physically, and it will also help them mentally focus. That last half hour before the race, it can be easy for an athlete to get "in their head" about the race. There are a hundred insecurities that can arise and cause the runner to lose focus. By giving them a highly structured pre-race plan and telling them that following this plan verbatim is their primary focus leading up to the race, you give them a feeling of control and a task to keep their mind occupied.

We recommend simple little note cards that list each aspect of their pre-race routine.
* Use the bathroom
* Walk/jog for 5 minutes
* 60/40s - provide specific number of sets
* Active stretching - list specific stretches
* Active drills - list specific drills
* 20/40/60/80s - provide specific number of sets
* Spike Up
* Check-In
* Race Time

Time out your warmup routines in practice to know exactly how long your runners take on each aspect of the warmup and then give them specific times for each activity, based on the expected start time of their race. The warmup routine is too important to leave it up to chance. Just a small amount of effort and organization by the coach will provide the structure the athletes need to properly prepare for their event.

High School Modifications:
Your warmup routine on meet day should be exactly like your warmup routine before a hard speed session in practice. One thing that is specific to high school coaches is the meet schedule. In college meets, there are often precise time schedules and meet officials stick to the schedule. In high school meets, there are often "rolling" schedules, which can make it difficult for the coach or athlete to know exactly when to begin the warmup. In those situations, I always gave athletes a specific event when they needed to begin their warmup, something that I calculated would be about 45–60 minutes before their race time. Instead of telling them to warm up at 6:15 precisely, I told them to begin warming up at the start of the 4x800 meter relay. Then if the meet did get behind schedule, their target event to begin the warmup was also behind schedule, so at least we did not have them warming up way too early.

Why This System Prevents Injury

The tough reality is that you can never prevent injuries 100% in any sport or in any running event. However, there are multiple reasons why this training program helps with injury prevention.

150 Meters is a Dangerous Distance
In our observation, many athletes who suffer injuries in practice do so in doing all-out running at prolonged or moderate distances. For example, injuries can easily occur when the athlete runs several all-out 150 meter repetitions with too much recovery time. When you ask the athlete to sprint all-out for that long while fatigued, you put their body at a higher likelihood of pulling a muscle. Most injuries that we have observed in workouts were running something similar to all out 150s.

Let us clarify a point here: We do a lot of fast running while tired. However, our fast running is much shorter—40 yards, 60 meters, distances like that. Very few muscle pulls occur in practice during a 5–6 second sprint. Most sprint injuries happen on the track because of all-out exertion at a distance that is too far for the athlete. You cannot get rid of sprinting and speed development, obviously you need to do that. We recommend running fast regularly in your training program, but try to minimize how *far* you are asking athletes to run all out.

Is It Really Speed Development?
We call this "prolonged sprinting," which is often a no-man's-land anyway. Consider this: If a runner hits top speed around 6 seconds, then what are you really accomplishing by doing all-out 150s? Instead, you should do one of two things. If you want to work on speed, do that in short bursts up to 6 seconds. If you want to work on endurance, do that by running longer repetitions. Repeat 150s do not accomplish speed development or endurance.

Strengthen the Hamstrings

One of the best things you can do with 400 meter runners (or any sprinter, really) is to help them strengthen their hamstring muscles. Many sprinters have strong quadriceps. These athletes have plenty of God-given fast twitch muscle fibers in their hamstrings, which is what makes them so fast in the first place, but they often have hamstrings that are relatively weaker than their quadriceps. This muscle imbalance is problematic, and when the athlete gets tired and they are still trying to run all out for prolonged sprints, this muscle imbalance often shows itself in the form of a hamstring cramp, strain, or pull.

We recommend half-squats and hamstring curls as two weight room lifts to do when trying to strengthen (or rehab) the hamstrings. With hamstring curls, the safest way to work the hamstrings is to do higher reps (20) at sub-max weight. Most hamstring issues are caused by fatigue. Your goal in the weight room should be to build muscular endurance, and you achieve this by lifting at sub-max weight and doing more repetitions. Fatiguing the hamstring is the key with hamstring curls.

When an athlete was returning from a hamstring injury, Coach Hart would make them do a maximum test on the hamstring curl. Once an athlete could lift 40 pounds with the injured hamstring they were allowed to return to training. Once the athlete could lift 60 pounds they were allowed to return to racing. These numbers would certainly be lower for high school athletes, but the principle here is that the athlete has to regain strength in that hamstring before they can go back to intense training and racing. Otherwise, they are just going to reinjure that muscle.

Chairs

Helping athletes improve their muscle flexibility is challenging. Most people are born with a certain amount of muscle flexibility and you can improve it as a coach, but usually not as much as you want to. Additionally, a majority of hamstring muscle pulls are on the sheathing of the muscle, which leaves behind scar tissue as it heals. Scar tissue has no elasticity, meaning that static stretching will not be helpful when dealing with a recovery from injury.

One of the best active stretches that we recommend to maintain hamstring flexibility before and during workouts is called *chairs*. Coach Hart learned this stretch from Ralph Mann, Olympic silver medalist in the 400 meter hurdles and Ph.D. and guru in the field of exercise biomechanics.

The instructions are pretty simple: Stand up with your feet shoulder width apart. Bend your knees, lean forward, and lower your body until you can grab both ankles with your hands. Keep hold of your ankles and slowly swing your hips up behind you until you feel your hamstrings straighten and stretch. Keep this slow and do it four times. This is a great, simple way to actively stretch your hamstrings. When you try to bend straight down to stretch your hamstrings, it does not work because you cannot stretch a muscle when it is tight.

Try this right now to prove our point: Without doing any stretching, try to bend straight down and touch your toes. Make a mental note of how far down you are able to reach. Now, do 4 sets of chairs and immediately after those sets try to reach down and touch your toes again. You should be able to reach an extra 1–2 inches because the chair stretch is actually stretching the muscle, not making it tighter. If you watch the video of the 1996 Olympic Trials, you will see Michael Johnson doing these chairs at the start line immediately before he broke the 200 meter world record.

We recommend doing these before each practice as part of your warmup routine, and we also suggest athletes do them periodically throughout a workout to keep those hamstrings loose. It is impossible to say for sure, but we believe that we have prevented many potential injuries with this one simple stretch. It takes less than a minute and you can do these at any point during the workout when you have standing recovery. It is a great safety precaution.

Core Strength

It might be obvious, but one of the key ways to prevent injuries is to develop strength in the core of the body (abdominal and back muscles) and to maintain proper balance between hamstring and quadriceps strength. There are a lot of different lifts and workouts that you can do in the weight room that will help athletes improve their core strength and balance in muscular strength. As a coach, make sure your athletes are regularly working on building their core strength.

Benediction

The word benediction typically carries with it a religious connotation. It is a prayer asking for divine favor or care for someone, typically issued when you depart from them. A pastor might issue the benediction at the end of a church service or a group of people might pray a benediction over a missionary who is about to travel overseas. This book is obviously not a religious book, but that is the best word that I could find to convey my wishes for you. If you are reading this, I hope the very best for you in all things.

The 400 is a beautiful race. There is good reason why the Greeks fell in love with this event nearly 3,000 years ago. Whether you are a coach, athlete, parent, or fan, I sincerely hope that this book provides you with helpful information about the 400 meter dash and how to properly train for and race this event.

If you would like to engage further in learning about the 400 meter dash, I invite you to visit my web site (www.400Wall.com) where we will continue this discussion.

References

Arcelli, E. (1995). Acido lattico e prestazione. *Palermo: Cooperativa Dante Editrice.*

Arcelli, E., Mambretti, M., Cimadoro, G., Alberti, G. (2008). The aerobic mechanism in the 400 metres. *New studies in athletics, 23*(2), 15–23.

Cicchella, A. (2022). The problem of effort distribution in heavy glycolytic trials with special reference to the 400 m dash in track and field. *Biology, 11*(2), 216.

Duffield, R., Dawson, B., & Goodman, C. (2004). Energy system contribution to 100-m and 200-m track running events. *Journal of Science and Medicine in Sport, 7*(3), 302–313.

Duffield, R., Dawson, B., & Goodman, C. (2005). Energy system contribution to 400-metre and 800-metre track running. *Journal of Sports Sciences, 23*(3), 299–307.

Hanon, C., & Gajer, B. (2009). Velocity and stride parameters of world-class 400-meter athletes compared with less experienced runners. *The Journal of Strength & Conditioning Research, 23*(2), 524–531.

Hill, D. W. (1999). Energy system contributions in middle-distance running events. *Journal of Sports Sciences, 17*(6), 477–483.

Lacour, J. R., Bouvat, E., & Barthelemy, J. C. (1990). Post-competition blood lactate concentrations as indicators of anaerobic energy expenditure during 400-m and 800-m races. *European Journal of Applied Physiology and Occupational Physiology, 61*(3–4), 172–176.

Martin, D. E., & Coe, P. N. (1997). *Better Training for Distance Runners.* Human Kinetics.

Newsholme, E. A., Blomstrand, E., & Ekblom, B. (1992). Physical and mental fatigue: metabolic mechanisms and importance of plasma amino acids. *British Medical Bulletin, 48*(3), 477–495.

Nummela, A., & Rusko, H. (1995). Time course of anaerobic and aerobic energy expenditure during short-term exhaustive running in athletes. *International Journal of Sports Medicine, 16*(08), 522–527.

Sökmen, B., Witchey, R. L., Adams, G. M., & Beam, W. C. (2018). Effects of sprint interval training with active recovery vs. endurance training on aerobic and anaerobic power, muscular strength, and sprint ability. *The Journal of Strength & Conditioning Research, 32*(3), 624–631.

Spencer, M. R., & Gastin, P. B. (2001). Energy system contribution during 200-to 1500-m running in highly trained athletes. *Medicine & Science in Sports & Exercise, 33*(1), 157–162.

USTFCCCA.org. Oliver Jackson, USTFCCCA coaches hall of fame class of 1997. Retrieved June 27, 2023, from https://www.ustfccca.org/awards/oliver-jackson-ustfccca-class-of-1997

van Ingen Schenau, G. J., Jacobs, R., & de Koning, J. J. (1991). Can cycle power predict sprint running performance? *European Journal of Applied Physiology and Occupational Physiology, 63*, 255–260.

van Someren, K. A. (2006). The physiology of anaerobic endurance training. *The Physiology of Training. UK: Churchill Livingstone*, 85–115.

Vilmi, N., Äyrämö, S., Nummela, A., Pullinen, T., & Linnamo, V. (2016). Oxygen uptake, acid-base balance and anaerobic energy system contribution in maximal 300–400 m running in child, adolescent and adult athletes. *Journal of Athletic Enhancement, 5*(3), 1–8.

Weyand, P. G., Cureton, K., Conley, D. S., & Sloniger, M. A. (1993). Percentage aerobic energy utilized during track running events. *Medicine and Science in Sports and Exercise, 25*(5), S105.

Weyand, P. G., Cureton, K., Conley, D. S., Sloniger, M. A., & Liu, Y. L. (1994). Peak oxygen deficit predicts sprint and middle-distance track performance. *Medicine and Science in Sports and Exercise, 26*(9), 1174–1180.

WorldAthletics.org. Retrieved June 27, 2023, from https://worldathletics.org/records/all-time-toplists/sprints/400-metres/outdoor/men/senior?regionType=world&timing=electronic&page=1&bestResultsOnly=false&firstDay=1899-12-30&lastDay=2023-06-26

Zwiren, L. D. (1989). Anaerobic and aerobic capacities of children. *Pediatric Exercise Science, 1*(1), 31–44.

Made in the USA
Columbia, SC
02 December 2024

48248355R00078